"All of Us"

By Brian Anderson

Foreward by Kelly Anderson

ISBN: 172272062X
ISBN-13: 978-1722720629

DEDICATION

For Kelly: You are the love of my life. We both know that none of this would have happened without you. I love you!

For Breah, Jared, Aiden, Alex, Kate, Trey, Joel, and Maddy: Each of you came to our family in your own way, but it was God's plan that each of you became an Anderson. I am thankful for God's plan…..

"Family isn't always blood. It's the people in your life who want you in theirs; the ones who accept you for who you are. The ones who would do anything to see you smile and who love you no matter what."

And, just in case you didn't know it, your mom and I love you all no matter what!

CONTENTS

PART 1: THE BIO FAMILY

PART 2: OUR INTERNATIONAL JOURNEY

PART 3: INTRO TO FOSTER CARE

PART 4: ADOPTION FROM FOSTER CARE

Acknowledgments

"God decided in advance to adopt us into his own family by bringing us to himself through Jesus Christ. This is what he wanted to do, and it gave him great pleasure." Ephesians 1:5 (New Living Translation)

PREFACE

As you read the pages that follow, it is my hope that you will read with an open mind and an open heart. This is the story of my family, which, you will find, is quite different from many other families. But, I am very confident that this is the story and fulfillment of God's plan for Kelly and I and our family.

My belief is that God has a plan for us all. This is an ideology that I frequently recite to my children. While we all may have plans of what we want to do in life or where we want to go, these plans need to be in line with God's plan for us as well. As Jeremiah 29:11 reminds us, "For I know the plans I have for you," declares the Lord, "plans to prosper you and not to harm you, plans to give you hope and a future."

The future that God had planned for Kelly and me is a future that I would never have envisioned. In fact, as you will see, it is a future that, had God not changed my heart, would never have happened. In retrospect, I now see that for many years I had a plan for my future. I had dreams, career goals and aspirations, things I wanted to accomplish, places I wanted to travel to, etc. All of these ambitions were not, in and of themselves, negatives. However, they shared a common goal of being what "I" wanted. Once God opened my eyes and changed my heart, I no longer

1

was concerned with what exactly it was that I wanted for my future. This became a turning point. With this change in perspective, my concerns started to center on what He wanted for me and for my family. As these changes took place, my goals, objectives, and ambitions changed as well.

The changes that have occurred, the things that have happened, the path that Kelly and I have traveled, and the family that God has blessed us with as a result of this turning point is truly amazing. It has not been accomplished through our own work or motives. There have been times when we both have wondered, "Is this you God?" or "Why is this happening, God?". It has not been easy, but it has been God's plan, and that is what matters.

So please understand, as you read this book, I am not advocating that everyone should become foster parents or adopt. What I am advocating for is that you play the role that you feel God is leading you to play. To that end, we can live in denial, as I did for quite some time, or we can take hold of His plan, and experience the joy of what is to come. We all have a role in caring for His children, no matter if they were born to us or to someone else. That is an undeniable fact.

"Pure and genuine religion in the sight of God the Father means caring for orphans and widows in their distress and refusing to let the world corrupt you." James 1:27

FOREWARD

I believe that everything happens for a reason. Even a broken leg happens for a reason. School was almost out and it was soon to be summer time. Sweet, sweet summertime. I could feel it in my veins! Like every other middle school student, I was beyond excited for summer break. Thoughts of trips to the pool with my friends, vacation, festivals, and fairs were on my summer bucket list. However, my true love was sports. I loved sports. At that time, I lived for sports. Sports were what I let define me. On the pitcher's mound I felt confident, accepted, and, to be honest, powerful. Those are all the things you want as a teenager confidence, acceptance, and power. My favorite sport was softball. There was not a camp around that I did not attend. A local eye doctor, Dr. Frank Tangeman, had coached me for several years. He, along with my parents, saw my love for pitching. Telling me to practice more was never a problem. Getting me to stop practicing was. I loved that sport more than anything.

School had been out for just a week and the summer of 1992 was in full swing. The weather was hot. I had begun my babysitting job, my softball team was having a winning season, and I loved seeing my name in the newspaper as winning pitcher for our parks and recreation league. In my selfish, middle school mind, I, at the time, felt like it was the Olympics.

3

Early that summer, on June 5th, I jumped out of bed. It was game day. Game days were the best days. I practiced and planned all day for that game under the lights at Mercelina Park. My parents always attended my games, but that night my brother Max also had a game. After supper, my parents said they were going to watch Max since we played at the same time. Coming from a family of four children it was not uncommon for them to split their time between us.

My game started, and after pitching a perfect inning, it was my turn to bat. I was batter number three. My best friend to this day, Kristin, was on first base and another teammate was on third. The count was full and I stroked a base hit which landed me on first. Being competitive, and I guess you can say greedy, that was not good enough for my over the top spirit. The next pitch, as soon as the ball went past the catcher, I took off to steal second base. At that time, I was running fast and felt as if I had plenty of time, then, at the last second, I heard my coach's voice say, "Get down!" As I slid into second base, something happened that would change me forever. My cleat got caught on the base and I began to feel the worst pain you can imagine. The second baseman gasped as she covered her mouth. The shortstop began screaming, "Her leg is laying the opposite way, oh my, it's broken so bad!" I looked down and through my pain and tears I could see the inner part of my ankle laying on top of the base in a twisted way no leg should ever be able to bend.

The intense softball game became quiet. Everyone was looking at me and whispering. I knew it was not good.

My pain was off the chart and I could hear the sound of the ambulance off in the distance. The paramedics scooped me up and at every bump, turn, or jolt, I felt it on the fifteen minute ride to the hospital. My parents arrived at the hospital just as the doctors were hanging up my x-rays. Doctors confirmed that I had a severe spiral fracture. It was something too complex for their small hospital. I was transferred to St. Rita's Medical Center for further treatment. I was filthy from lying in the dirt, and the pain medicine they gave me only took my pain from a ten to a nine so I was still in an insane amount of pain. The hour drive to the next hospital was grueling to say the least. I remember crying out to God saying, "Why God, why me? What have I done to deserve this?" I remember being so mad, frustrated, and worried all at once. All my summer plans were down the drain. My love for playing softball was still there, but I knew I would not see that mound anytime soon. My faithful Mom fell asleep next to my bed that night in a recliner. We were sharing a room with several other kids. One was a little African American girl who had sickle cell anemia. The nurses were in taking care of her and I remember asking, "Where is her mom?" A nurse replied that this girl's mother was not present because she was actually in foster care. My heart started to ache for her. "How in world could any mother not be there for their sick child", I thought. I started to wonder what was going to happen to this little girl? Where were her foster parents? Why would God give her to a woman or parents that didn't take care of her? Something happened to me that night. I began to feel less sorry for myself and more sorry for her. I also started to question God and wonder why he let bad things happen to good people. At that time I did not understand. My mom would say over and over again, "Everything happens for a reason. We may not know why today or tomorrow, but I promise someday we will." Little did I know how true my mother's words would play out in my life. Moms are always right!

My parents, grandparents, friends, and siblings did all they could to entertain me that summer. The truth was, I was growing more depressed by the day. I had a cast from my foot to my thigh and I was confined to moving about in a wheel chair. Sitting and watching was not my thing. As much time as I had previously invested in practice, it still would not make up for the year that I had ahead of me to heal. As a fourteen year old, I was in a dark place. Clearly I was not living with purpose. I was going through the motions.

The next summer I had intended on getting back into sports, returning to softball, and taking my place upon the pitcher's mound again. Though I had recently been cleared to play again, the truth was I still had a very weak, skinny leg and a fear of suffering the same sort of injury again. Physically and mentally, I was no longer at 100%.

A pastor of our church at the time, Brian Graham, along with my uncle Jerry, encouraged me to attend a mission trip in Haiti that summer. They said we would spend two weeks caring for sick, orphaned children and running a Bible School for the healthy orphaned children. Again, I was young, selfish, and depressed. I began to have thoughts that I already lost my previous summer, so why would I want to waste another summer helping kids I didn't even know. However, softball was not going so well, so I agreed to leave my small town summer plans. Brian Graham told me, "If you let go and let God, He will use you," followed by, "Kelly, I promise this trip will change your life." Brian Graham was correct!

On the plane ride to Haiti, I was a cluster of emotions. I was happy, excited, nervous, scared, and mostly confused. I remember praying on that plane for God to use me. "Help me to know your purpose for my life," I prayed. Then, I remember wondering if God was even listening. I was a fourteen year old, bratty teenager with zits on her face and major attitude. What in the world was I even doing going to Haiti to help children? I needed help myself.

As I stepped off the plane in Haiti, everything about my attitude changed. The sights were more than my fourteen year old eyes would have ever imagined. I was in the midst of poverty. Men and women were walking the streets nude. Children were begging for food. People were literally dying in front of me in the villages. My leg injury and all my teenage concerns suddenly became so minor. I was so angry at myself for letting it take a year of my joy. There was so much more to live for, so much more to be concerned about than softball, my friends, and what was happening Friday night.

I watched as children were eating off the ground. I experienced grown women trying to hand me their newborn babies, begging me to take care of them. Young children were walking for miles, barefoot, in hope of obtaining some food and water. God was opening my eyes. My soul was beginning to change. It didn't take long till it dawned on me, "This was exactly why I broke my leg so badly." God wanted me to slow down, refocus, and start living with purpose. God had called me to love and care for orphans. My heart was beating out of my chest and my love for these children was exploding.

The trip went so fast. I never wanted to leave. There were so many orphaned children, I wanted to take them all home and be a voice for them. One night, while still in Haiti, we stood in a group with hundreds of homeless children singing Amazing Grace. Every pot-bellied, lice infested child around me was singing and smiling. They had so much joy. They were so resilient. Every child was thankful for what they had, which was very little. These sweet angels began to hold my hand, and soon after, I found myself holding a little girl around the age of five. She smelled of urine, head lice had made a home in her short, black curly hair, and her belly was distended due to extreme starvation. For some reason, I was not worried about the smell of urine, her distended stomach, or the fact that the lice could exit her hair and enter mine. I knew, in this moment, I was exactly where God wanted me. The trip was coming to a close and my heart was ripping out of my chest. I wanted to stay. I had fallen in love for the first time in my life. I was in love with the children of Haiti.

Once I arrived home, everything seemed different. Never again did I take food for granted. My warm house in the winter and cool house in the summer was appreciated more. Of course, as a teenager, I wanted name brand clothing and nice things, but if I didn't have them, then that was okay as well. I spent my next school year going through the motions until I could return to the mission field the following summer. I spent my babysitting money and waitressing money sponsoring children through the Compassion Child Organization. The reading I did became adoption related. I played sports, but mostly for fun. When our soccer team lost the championship game, I was not crying on the bus with my teammates. In the back of my mind lingered the faces of the children in Haiti that had lost so much more than a soccer game. And the thing was, these children, despite their circumstances, were still smiling. I realized that a soccer game was just that.....a soccer game!

My sophomore year, I started dating Brian Anderson. He was in the top ten of our class and a great basketball player. Most importantly he was kind, fun, and handsome! Brian and I were high school sweethearts. Like many young couples, we had some break ups and set-backs, but we always ended up back together. Brian and I married a year after we graduated when I was 19 and Brian was 20. Everyone thought we were crazy. We were young and in love and there was just no separating us. A few days after Brian asked me to marry him I told him, "We really need to talk." He looked at me kind of worried. Brian listened to me that night as I shared with him that I wanted to adopt someday. It was something that I wanted to make sure he was on board with because it was what I knew I was called to do. Brian was well aware of my love for orphans. I just wanted to make sure he knew I was serious because I knew that God would never want me to marry a man who was not in agreement. Brian agreed that he was interested and would be open to it someday. We were married on August 16, 1997.

I knew that in order to adopt internationally you had to be married for five years in many cases. Brian had also shared with me that he wanted at least two biological children as well. About six months after we were married, we were expecting our first child. Breah Ashtyn Anderson was born a week before Christmas in 1998. Jared Joseph Anderson was born in July of 2000. Aiden Joseph Anderson arrived in March of 2003. Brian and I decided, after three children in five years, and very rough pregnancies for me, we were done having biological children. As Aiden was approaching his first birthday, I started bringing up adoption to Brian. I reminded him of our conversation before we were married. He started to back-peddle. His common answer was to say, "We have our hands full," or, "adoption is so expensive." Sometimes he would respond, "Do you really want to still do that?"

My heart was breaking. I felt like this man, who I was madly in love with, was backing out and breaking promises. Did he really just tell me he was ok with adoption to shut me up? It didn't take long, and I started to think maybe I was crazy for still wanting to adopt. I had three beautiful, healthy children, a husband who loved me, and I was wanting to adopt children from across the world. I was back to where I was as a fourteen year old, questioning God. Yet, at the end of every day, I knew beyond the shadow of a doubt there was a child out there that was meant to be in our family.

CHAPTER 1

A SEED PLANTED

In the early spring of 1994, I met the woman who would forever change my life. As the story has played out she has also changed many more lives than mine.

Kelly Westerfield, as I knew her then, was my soul mate. I may not have known this at first, but it did not take all that long for me to figure it out. We were the typical high school sweethearts. You know, the ones that you hear about every now and then that stay together through high school then go to college and no one ever really knows what happens after that. Well, I was determined that we would be different. We would be the ones that stayed together and someday, we would be able to tell our children and grandchildren about our story.....how we were the high school sweethearts that made it.

I now know this is not the story we will tell our children and grandchildren. Being high school sweethearts will not define us. My wife has seen to that. The story we will tell to anyone who will listen, and a theme of this book, is the story of how perseverance pays off. It is the story of how sometimes you need to block out the noise that life throws at you and listen to that still, small voice that tugs at your heart. It is the story of following God's plan, rather than our own. It is the story of how having faith means giving up control. It is the story of how love can change everything. It is the story of realizing how much more there is to life when you realize it is not "things" that make life great, but the lives you can touch that makes life worth living. It is the story of how a family can be built from miscellaneous parts and pieces that have been discarded by others, and that these parts can be mended, rearranged, and fit together to make the family unit stronger. The story we have told our children, will tell our grandchildren, and will tell anyone who will listen, is the story of adoption and fostering and adopting again, because that is how the Anderson family has been built. My wife has seen to that.

Our journey has been a team effort, but it started a long time ago. Kelly has had a heart for children in need since before we were a team. I remember long talks during our high school years. For some reason, many of these talks would incorporate the topic of adoption and how some day Kelly's dream was to adopt a child. As any good high school boyfriend would do, I would nod my head in agreement and say something intelligent like, "Yeah, that would be neat". Our relationship grew, and these talks would still pop up from time to time. We were married in 1997, and still, my persistent wife would occasionally bring up the subject of adopting. By this time, my answer had changed to, "Let's have some children first, then we can think about that". I was dragging my feet. She knew it.

We were blessed with our first child, Breah in 1998. Jared was born in the summer of 2000. Aiden came along in the spring of 2003. Now, not only was I dragging my feet on the whole adoption thing, I was starting to dig my heels in. After all, we now had three small children to care for, right? Our hands were full the way it was. It wasn't that I didn't care about children who needed a family. It was just that I couldn't wrap my head around the concept of adoption. I had too many questions for which I didn't know the answers. What if the birth mother or father would come back and try to take their child away from us? What about all the costs associated with adoption and how do we pay for that? What if some day my child says to me, "You're not even my real dad." What will our biological children think about an adopted sibling? These trivial things were roadblocks only because I had allowed them to be.

If Kelly had allowed me, I believe I would still be dragging my feet to this very day. But that is not my wife. She finally gave me the push I needed in the winter of 2003. Unbeknownst to me, she booked us a little get away. She told me that we needed a weekend away from the kids. I agreed. As we were driving to Cleveland, Ohio, for our getaway that cold winter day, she filled me in on the rest of the story. You see, the hotel that we were staying at was actually next to a convention center where there was a weekend adoption convention. Coincidence? No, it wasn't. Kelly had already purchased our tickets to the convention.

The rest is history now. It is the story of our family. It is what defines us. My attendance at that convention on a snowy day in the winter of 2003, is what I needed to block out the noise and tear down the roadblocks so that I could listen to that still, small voice tugging at my heart. Kelly's persistence won out. God's calling for our family could now proceed. The Anderson expansion had begun.

Kelly is the love of my life, my best friend. She is an unwavering mother to our children. She puts our family first and herself last. We are a team, but she is also the coach and general manager. God is the architect of our family; Kelly is the job site foreman who sees that everything is in place and done right. When things in our family start to fall apart, she is the glue that puts them back together. She has a heart for children in need of forever families. I have learned so much from just watching her care for, nurture, and strive to fix their damaged lives every single day.

It is my hope that as you progress through the following pages, that you will attempt to block out the noise in your own life. I challenge you to read this story and ask yourself if you have heard that still, small voice. If so, have you listened? Or have you pushed it aside as I did for many years? I will be the first to say, if not for my wife's persistence and her intent to follow what she knew was God's calling, I would have missed out. Our family would not be the same, which really raises some serious questions that I don't even want to consider. While your calling may not be the same as my family's, I believe that everyone has a part to play because there are so many children out there who need love, care, someone to be their advocate, and sometimes, a forever family.

Adopting one child will not change the world. But for that one child, it will change the world forever.

CHAPTER 2

THE BEGINNING OF OUR FAMILY

In telling our story, I would be remiss to gloss over the backstory and its associated details. As I have referenced before, Kelly and I were high school sweethearts. We got married just over a year after graduating high school. We were young when we decided to start our forever journey together.

We also became young parents. Breah Ashtyn, our oldest daughter, was born on December 18, 1998, when I was just 21 and Kelly was 20. I remember Breah's birth like it was yesterday. I was a young, proud father. I remember crying at her birth as I experienced the joy of becoming a first time father. I never could have imagined the sheer joy that becoming a parent would bring to my life.

Breah, from a very young age, was always so mature that it amazed me. As a young toddler, Kelly and I would always joke that she was like a little bird – always looking to see what was happening around her. She always wanted to be held. She was extremely social, a child who could not stand to be in a different room than where the action was occurring. She was fiercely independent, the type of child who wanted to do everything herself, with you watching, of course. It is strange how these traits that we noticed early on have stayed consistent as she has grown older.

Breah now, is a fiercely independent young woman, 19 years of age. She is still a person who is comfortable in any social setting. Put her in a room full of strangers, and by the end of the night, she will have made a group of new friends. She is self-motivated and has career goals and aspirations including plans of someday going to law school. She is unafraid of new experiences. She is a bird ready to spread her wings and fly, as evidenced by her heading out west where she attends the University of Wyoming, just over 1,200 miles away from her home town.

The traits described above have served to make Breah a strong, passionate young woman whom Kelly and I are extremely proud of. These traits have also made Breah a sound role model for all of our children. She has been instrumental in varying ways over the years as our family has grown. Breah traveled with us to Korea when she was just 6 years old to pick up Alex. When we brought Alex home, Breah served as the "mother hen" for him. For some time, as Alex got to know us, Breah served as Kelly's right hand in caring for Alex, as he initially liked her much more than me. Whatever role our family has needed Breah to fill, she has always been able. From babysitter to big sister, from changing diapers to helping potty train, from helping with homework to being a family taxi cab, she has done it all.

On July 12, 2000, Kelly and I welcomed the next member of our family to this world. Jared Joseph (Jay) was born suddenly, and by suddenly, I mean we almost didn't get to the hospital in time. At the time, I was working as a Firefighter/Paramedic with the Celina Fire Department. The day of Jay's birth, I was supposed to be home from work shortly after 6 pm. As fate would have it, we had a run at the end of the shift that evening, causing me to be late. What I didn't know as I went out on that run, was that Kelly knew it was "time" to go to the hospital. What Kelly didn't know was that I was going to be late. As I arrived home that evening, I was met by Kelly who had already taken Breah to the babysitter. Kelly let me know it was time to go, so as we drove the 15 minute drive to the hospital, I became the "coach" telling her that we had time….that it was going to be alright. Standing in the hospital lobby, Kelly's water broke, and we were rushed back to the OB unit as her contractions were getting stronger and closer together with each passing minute.

Jay was born shortly after we arrived that night. As Kelly's nurse midwife ran into the room, throwing on her gown, with just enough time to glove one hand; Jay entered this world. As he did, it was noted that he was not breathing well, so he was whisked away to the waiting resuscitation nurses. Kelly and I really did not have any chance to see him at first. After a few minutes under the warming lap and with some breathing assistance, Jay pinked up and took off like a newborn should. I was the first to see him. He had no hair, an odd shaped head, a barrel chest, and the longest arms and fingers I had ever seen on a baby. As I returned to Kelly, she asked if Jay was okay. I told her that he was; that all was well. She then asked me the question I was hoping she would skip. "Is he cute?" Kelly asked. I was honest with her, as I informed her, "He looks like ET." Fortunately, as he grew into a toddler, he became a handsome young boy with blond hair, brown eyes, and glasses.

From a young age, Jay has been very resilient and content. I remember him as a toddler. He was the type of kid that could be in a room by himself, and as long as he had something close to occupy his time, he didn't have a worry in the world. In some ways, he was the opposite of Breah. He was very content to just be left alone. He would take naps in his crib, wake up, and not make a sound for an hour after, because he was content just playing there by himself. As he grew, he maintained his resilience and independence. When he would get new toys, he always wanted to be the one to read the directions and put them together himself. It has always been evident that he is a very methodical and analytical type of person. Jay enjoys the process and challenges of learning.

Jay has grown into a young man that Kelly and I couldn't be more proud of. He is intelligent and continues to be very analytical. At times, I find him quizzing me on the "why" of things, which is at the same time challenging and rewarding as a parent. Jay loves the outdoors and hunting, and is the reason why I now love to hunt (thank you Jay!). Jay is the "big brother" of our family, not just in name or birth order, but in action as well. If something around the house isn't done correctly, he will make sure to point it out to one of his siblings, but he is also willing to help show and teach how to do it correctly. Like Breah, Jay is also very self-motivated, with plans to attend college majoring in a medical field, and further aspirations to proceed to medical school and become a doctor.

In April of 2001, Kelly told me that she was expecting again. We were excited. Our plan was to have our children all close together in age, and it was progressing nicely. However, on Jay's first birthday, at about 13 weeks into her pregnancy, Kelly experienced a miscarriage. While this was a difficult time in our life, we also knew that this child of ours was in heaven. Kelly and I are firm believers that life begins at conception, so, with that belief, we are confident that we will someday meet this child of ours. After Kelly's miscarriage, we put our family planning on hold for a while. We had discussed having three children, but this threw us an unexpected curveball. Kelly, with each pregnancy, had had a very rough go of it, so this was a time when Kelly started to bring up the topic of adoption. I, of course, was very much against taking that route at the time.

As God had planned, Kelly would have one more child naturally. On March 13, 2003, Aiden Joseph came into this world. Aiden was a chubby little newborn with thick, dark hair. Aiden was a rude awakening for us, as he was nothing like what we had experienced with Breah and Jay. Aiden was a cranky, pukey, discontented baby. Aiden always wanted held and, when held, frequently still wasn't happy. We laugh about this because that mentality is the total opposite of Aiden's personality now as a young teen.

Aiden is one of the kindest young men you could ever meet. He is the type that would give someone the shirt off his own back if he knew it would help them. Aiden has a caring, compassionate heart. He has been to Haiti with Kelly, and longs to go back so that he can help make a difference in children's lives. He has a heart for children, which is evident in his daily interactions with his younger siblings. Aiden also has a laid back, carefree attitude, and I mean this in a good way. He doesn't get upset about the little things in life. Even as a young teen, I believe he realizes and prioritizes what is important in life. Aiden has found that he loves making videos, and has actually become quite good at it – (check him out on YouTube at AidenAnderVlogs, and please like and subscribe) – to the point of considering "vlogging" as a career (that is for you Jay). With that said, I have informed him (and Jay has as well) that if the YouTube career doesn't work out, he needs to have a back-up plan, so Aiden also talks about becoming a flight attendant as a career. I think he would make an excellent flight attendant, and I know he would love the travel.

So there you have it…..besides Kelly and I, these are the first three members of the Anderson family. If it isn't evident by what I have written about each one, I am a very proud parent. Breah, Jay, and Aiden all have outstanding personality traits, career goals and aspirations, and values. I thank God every day for everyone one of my children, and these three are where it all started.

Our family journey has not been solely through the efforts of Kelly and me alone. Breah, Jay, and Aiden have been an active part of every step. At all points, we have held open, honest family discussions with our children about where we felt God was leading us and what our intentions were. We have asked them questions, and attempted, to the best of our ability, to answer any questions that they may have had. Of course, when Breah, Jay, and Aiden were younger, these discussions were not nearly as in depth as they have been over the last couple years. But as our family has grown, so have the strength, maturity, and understanding of Breah, Jay, and Aiden. I am confident that they have seen that following God's plan, while not always easy, is always the right thing to do.

From time to time, as in many families, we will have discussions with our children about what they think that their future may hold. Many times, in these discussions, the question will come up, "How many children do you think you will have?" Breah, Jay, and Aiden frequently state they believe they will have some biological children as well as adopted children. As a parent, this means the world to me. They have been a part of God's plan for our family, they have seen it work, and they realize that as a family, we have been called to care for children. I hope and pray that as they continue to grow into adulthood and have families of their own, they will continue to listen to God's calling for their lives and families, whatever that may be.

CHAPTER 3

A CHANGE OF HEART

So, there we were in March of 2003. I was happily married to the love of my life and my best friend. We had three children that we loved dearly. Little did I know at the time, the same year just 6 months after Aiden, our next child would be born.

With Kelly's rough pregnancies, we had decided that Aiden would be our last child. Hold on, let me rephrase that......with Kelly's rough pregnancies, I had decided that Aiden would be our last child. What Kelly had decided, without my knowledge at the time, was that while Aiden would be her last child that she gave birth to, she had no intention for him to be our last child. When Aiden was about 6 months old, Kelly's thoughts and plans for the future started to become evident to me.

In the fall of 2003, the topic of adoption again became a frequent conversation in our family. As I have related previously, I was against adopting. I found every excuse that I could as reason to NOT adopt. Kelly would frequently pass me articles and books about adoption. I would say that I was going to read them, but I wouldn't. I was stubborn. Kelly was persistent.

The winter of that year was when a change would happen in my life. Under the guise of a "weekend away for just us......because we need it", Kelly got me up to Cleveland to attend an adoption conference being held at the convention center there. I remember approaching this weekend with large amounts of skepticism, after all, I already had my mind made up that there were too many obstacles in the road in order for adoption to be an option for our family. Kelly, on the other hand, was excited. All she had done since her first mission trip to Haiti as a young teenager was feel the calling to adopt, and now, despite the trickery involved with getting me to go, she had us both registered to attend this adoption conference.

While I don't remember all the specifics of this conference, what I do remember to this very day is the change that God started to facilitate within me that weekend. This conference was absolutely not what I expected. We had opportunities to speak with families who had adopted, to hear their stories – the good and the bad parts included, and to ask questions during small group breakout sessions. It didn't take long before I started feeling differently about the thought of adoption and the concept as it applied to Kelly and me and to our family.

At the end of the first day of this conference, I was intrigued. By the end of the second day of this conference, I was hooked. To go from one end to the polar opposite end of the spectrum with regard to my openness to becoming an adoptive parent, well, that is what happened

24

over the course of these two days. It is a change that can only be explained by barriers inside me being broken down. My wife, her persistence, and her prayers were the facilitator, but I have no doubt that God was the ultimate force that caused my eyes to be opened to His calling for our family. I remember leaving our weekend in Cleveland, asking myself, "How could I have been so blind to God's calling to take care of these children in need of families?" I vividly remember a statement that an adoptive parent made in one of the sessions we had attended that weekend. "How can someone profess to be pro-life, but anti-adoption?", they said. This question stuck with me as we traveled back home, and has stuck with me to this very day. I was absolutely pro-life, however, I always thought that someone else should step up to take care of children in need of families. After all, I was too busy. We had three children already. What if, what if, what if? Excuse after excuse was all I had ever made when confronted with the concept of adoption. As we headed back home, this question played over and over in my head, and my excuses to not adopt melted away. I had heard God's calling many times through my wife, but now I was ready to listen to His call.

Back in Celina, Kelly was excited. I was now a willing participant in this proposed adoption journey. But, how does one start such a journey? Fortunately, during the preceding months, my wife had been vigorously exploring our options. After some discussion and prayer, we felt that we were being directed to pursue international adoption. I can remember many nights, Kelly sitting in front of the computer for hours studying the adoption process for many different countries. I remember her looking at listing after listing. It was eye opening to me as I started to realize the enormous number of children in need of a forever family.

As we started to zero in on possibilities, I remember specifically telling Kelly that I wanted to adopt a girl. At that time, our family consisted of two boys and only one girl, so I thought it was important to make sure that Breah had a sister. Kelly and I continued to research and started to focus in on adoption possibilities from China. However, we soon found out that we were not "candidates" for adoption from China due to their requirements that both parents were at least 30 years of age. At the time, I was 26 and Kelly was 25. We looked at Ukraine as a possibility, but ultimately decided against it because of the requirement of multiple visits to the country, which we couldn't afford.

This process went on week after week. We researched, we looked, and we researched some more. As this cycle continued, quite honestly, it started to feel overwhelming. But, one night, things started to take shape. Kelly, while completing her nightly routine of adoption research, found a picture of a little boy named Seung Joon Ha. He had been born in September of 2003, in South Korea, just six months after Aiden had been born to us. The blurb of an update that was available on him stated that he was preparing to have open heart surgery and that he was in need of a forever family. As his eyes stared out from the computer screen at her, Kelly knew that Seung Joon Ha was the one. Now she just had to convince me.

The next day, Kelly brought me to the computer to show me what she had found the night before. My first reaction was, "I thought we agreed on wanting a sister for Breah." Kelly assured me that we had agreed, but that there was something inside her telling her to find out more about this little boy with big brown eyes and long black hair. We contacted the international adoption agency that had his listing. We requested more information. We found out that he was now 6 months old, that he had had successful open heart surgery, and that his adoption referral had been declined by over 15 families due to his history of congenital heart defects.

We talked, we prayed, and we talked some more, but Kelly's conviction that this little boy was meant to be in our family became my conviction as well. We signed up with the agency that had his listing, we obtained our home study, and we received his entire case file. Seung Joon Ha had been born with an atrial septal defect and a ventricular septal defect, basically meaning he had two holes in the lining separating chambers within his heart. We were informed that per the documentation from South Korea, these had been fixed during his open heart surgery. We were also advised that Seung Joon had been born with a condition called dextrocardia, meaning his heart was on the right side of his chest rather than the normal left side placement. With my background as a paramedic, I immediately started researching dextrocardia. It quickly became evident that in some cases dextrocardia was a very minor issue, but in other cases it was associated with other heart defects that could involve major surgeries and/or complications. Based on the information we had from his file, where Seung Joon's condition fell in the spectrum was a total unknown. Despite the questions that loomed around

27

this medical history, Kelly and I had peace. We both felt that God was telling us this was the child that He intended to be in our family. With that being the case, we proceeded down the path to be matched with and adopt little Seung Joon Ha from Busan, South Korea.

CHAPTER 4

SEUNG JOON HA

International adoption is a journey. Our initial steps in this journey involved paperwork, and a lot of it. There are forms to fill out, background checks to be done, fingerprints to be completed, US visa applications to be submitted. There are literally mountains of forms to complete. So, after accepting the referral of Seung Joon Ha, this was our task for the next few months. As with many things in life, there are also delays, waiting periods, and hurdles that have to be crossed in order for the paperwork of international adoption to get where it needs to go.

As we completed this tedious process, week by week, we waited for updates on Seung Joon. These updates were few and far between, which, of course, made the process seem like it was taking even longer. Having a child half way across the world, knowing that they are your child, but yet, not being able to have and hold them is a tough thing to do for any period of time, let alone almost 12 months. That was our time frame. From first seeing this little boy on a computer screen, to our date of travel, was just over a year.

In deciding how we would get Seung Joon home, we had two options. We could pay for a Korean case worker to fly with him to Detroit, where we would be waiting at the airport for the handoff, or we could travel to South Korea ourselves to pick up our son. Kelly and I both knew that this would be a turbulent time for the boy that we had decided to name "Alex". There was about to be a big change in his life. We also knew that if we traveled overseas, we would be able to experience his home country and culture. We would be afforded the opportunity to introduce ourselves to Alex on a more gradual basis, and we would get to meet Alex's foster parents. Considering all of those things, we thought it best that we travel to South Korea ourselves to meet Alex and bring him home.

As we approached the twelve month time frame, with all paperwork, forms, passports, and visas in hand, we were finally given a date for our trip to South Korea to pick up our son. Our travel was set for the last week in March in 2005. Alex was 18 months old.

Leaving for Korea was an exciting experience. Looking back now, I would equate it to a feeling like a child waiting for Christmas. The anticipation, the excitement, the questions, and the joy that was felt as our travel date approached was a breath of fresh air after months and months of waiting. As we boarded the plane, with Breah, who was 6 at the time, and my sister Emily, who was 12, none of us knew what to expect. Our flight from Chicago to Seoul lasted just over 16 hours, but, amazingly enough, seemed like it was over in the blink of an eye. Emily, thinking she was eating some sort of oriental fresh fruit, tasted sushi for the first time – and didn't like it. We all laughed, joked, talked about what we expected Korea to be like, napped, and finally arrived at Incheon International Airport in Seoul.

Having never been international travelers, when we arrived in Seoul, we fumbled our way through customs, we exchanged US dollars for Korean won, we grabbed our luggage, and we met up with our ride – a driver from the Eastern Social Welfare Society (the Korean agency whom we were adopting through), who would take us to their orphanage where we were staying during our time in Seoul. The trip from the airport to where we were staying lasted about 45 minutes, all of which we spent staring out the windows of the van, transfixed, just taking in the sights of this country and city. To give you an idea, for comparison, Chicago has a current population of about 2.7 million people in the city itself and slightly less than 10 million people in the metropolitan area, while Seoul has a city population of about 10 million people with approximately 25 million people living in the metropolitan area. None of us had ever seen anything like this before.

Eastern Social Welfare Society is a South Korean agency that was founded by Pastor Kim Duk-Hwang in 1971. Through his efforts to establish and develop this agency, Eastern now provides a wide range of services including education and special education services, support for single mothers and the elderly, medical services, residential assistance, job training and assistance, and adoption services for children needing forever families.

It was evening when we arrived at Eastern Social Welfare Society's main building. We were scheduled to meet Alex and his foster mother for the first time the following day, so in the meantime, we decided to walk and explore. Seoul was like nothing we had ever experienced. Seoul has a smell all its own, enhanced by the smell of Asian spices from the food vendors that can be found all over street corners and alley ways. The people were friendly and extremely helpful when needed. As westerners who were obviously out of their comfort zone, we quickly found that the people of Seoul were eager to help, and if able to converse in English, eager to hold a conversation. We stayed out late that night, but felt safe the entire time, highlighting another aspect of the Asian culture that we quickly noticed as we experienced Seoul. As a city of almost 10 million people, the subway system is vast, enabling travel to anywhere in the city, however, not once in our entire time in Seoul, did we ever see one glimpse of graffiti. It was very evident from the beginning of our trip that the atmosphere here exemplified respect. This respectfulness was on display for all to see in the manner in which public property was treated and maintained.

The next day, we met Alex and his foster mother for the first time. The plan was that each day for increasing amounts of time, we would get to meet and interact with Alex and his foster mother. That being the case, this first visit lasted about one hour, and, despite our best efforts, Alex wanted nothing to do with us! It was easy to see the bond and attachment that was present between Alex and his foster mother. Since Alex was born, this woman had been there for him. Through his open heart surgery and his recovery in the hospital, this woman was by his side. Alex loved her, and while at that first visit he was willing to take a little toy fire truck from Kelly and me, he was not willing to go any further than that.

Each day for the next two days, we got to spend a little more time with Alex and his foster mother. At each visit, Eastern provided a bilingual case worker so that we could talk with and get to know his foster mother, who could then tell us all about Alex, his likes, his dislikes, and any other information she felt important to provide prior to Alex leaving Korea with us. This experience was truly a joy for both Kelly and me, but as the week progressed, we continued to see just how much Alex loved his foster mother. This woman, who had fostered over 30 children before Alex, told us the story of our little boy in the hospital before, during, and after surgery. She told us how she worried that he might not make it. After he was sent home from the hospital, she told us how she worried that he might not find a forever family because of his heart condition. You see, at 18 months of age, he was by far the longest foster placement she had ever had. She told us how much she loved Seung Joon Ha, and how she was so happy that he now had a family.

For our part, Kelly and I repeatedly thanked her for all the information, for loving Alex, and for caring for him for the first, and probably the most difficult, part of his life. Each night, when we would return to our room at Eastern, we would talk about how difficult this transition would be for Alex and for his foster mother. We saw the bond and attachment between them. It was undeniable. This weighed heavily upon Kelly and me. We started to question, "Is this adoption what is best for Alex?" Leading up to the day that we would take Alex back to the United States, we had a discussion with our Korean case worker, in which we asked if there was any chance that Alex's foster mother could ever adopt him or keep him permanently. We were told that, no, this was not an option. I can say to this day without a doubt, the love and bond was so strong between Alex and his foster mother, that if she would have been able to keep and raise him, Kelly and I both would have left South Korea without him.

As we approached the end of the week, on Thursday, we spent the entire day with Alex and his foster mother. We visited the hospital in Seoul where his open heart surgery had been performed. We met Alex's cardiologist. We visited Alex's foster mother's home and we met Alex's foster father and his foster sister, as he was not the only foster child in the house. We heard stories of how Alex's foster father, a taxi driver, would take Alex for rides in his car when Alex was cranky, because this seemed to soothe him. We laughed, we cried, we thanked, and we hugged. As happy as we were, this was a difficult day, because Kelly and I knew at the end of the day, Alex would not be going back home with his foster mother. Rather, he would be returning with Kelly and me to our room at Eastern Social Welfare Society.

As the time neared for this "handoff" to occur, Pastor Kim, the founder of Eastern Social Welfare Society, came down and prayed with us all. Tears flowed for

34

various reasons, some parts joy, some parts sadness, some parts relief, and some parts out of realization that a bond was about to be severed and a new bond was about to begin. Thankfully, Alex fell asleep during this time, which made the handoff proceed more smoothly. As we parted ways with Alex's foster mother, through her tears, she asked us to love him and take care of him. Kelly and I promised that we would. That day, we also promised that we would do whatever we could to someday bring Alex back to Seoul to meet his amazing foster mother. She said she would love that very much, she thanked us for making Alex a part of our family, and crying, she walked out the door.

Despite being happy to finally have our son and being ready to return home, that night was terrible. I will never claim to have any clue as to what our 18 month old son may have been thinking, suffice it to say, he wasn't happy. He spoke Korean, we did not. We looked different, smelled different, talked different, and at that time, in his mind, we weren't his mom or dad. We cushioned the blow a little bit by taking him out to eat that evening at, what we would discover, must have been one of his most favorite Korean restaurants – Pizza Hut. I have never seen a little guy eat so much pizza. It was amazing, and this experience of "new" food – food that he obviously loved – did well to soothe him for a little while. But, back at Eastern for our last night in Seoul, Alex cried for his "eomma" – his mother.

The flight home was much the same. Here Kelly and I were, an American couple bringing home a little

Asian boy, who obviously was not happy to be with us. Alex cried, he threw fits, he vomited. It was not the picture perfect journey back home that we had always imagined, but it was real. Thankfully, we had booked our flight tickets with Korean Air, so all of the flight attendants were bilingual Koreans. Frequently on our trip back to Chicago, these young ladies would carry Alex around with them, singing to him and speaking to him softly in Korean. Every time they did this, Alex would seem to calm down and relax. To this day, I have no clue what exactly it was that they would say to him, but they assured Kelly and I that they understood what was going on and were trying to calm his anxiety, assuring him that he was with his new "eomma" and "appa" – mommy and daddy.

By the time our flight arrived back in Chicago, Alex had warmed a little to Kelly. This would be a theme for at least the next couple years, as he quickly became a mommy's boy. We then flew from Chicago to Dayton, Ohio, where we were met by our other children, members of our family, and some friends. Everyone was so excited to meet Alex, and I remember Alex just wanted to latch onto Kelly. When I think about it, I can't imagine what could have been going on in his little mind at that time. As we drove home from Dayton, sitting in car seats next to each other, Alex and Aiden, who are only 6 months apart in age, interacted together for the first time. It was on that car ride home where Aiden, who had just turned two years old and had given up having a bottle months earlier, regressed somewhat, needing the comfort of a bottle just like Alex. As we finally arrived home and pulled into our driveway, I looked back and saw Breah smiling at her new brother, Jay watching his new brother intently, like he was studying him, and Aiden and Alex scowling at each other, seemingly racing to see who could finish their "bobby" first.

CHAPTER 5

ALEX JOSEPH ANDERSON

Alex came home on March 25, 2005. With adoption rules and requirements being what they were, we had to have Alex in our care for at least 6 months prior to finalizing his adoption. Under the guidance of a young, new attorney and family friend, Ross Finke, we finalized his adoption on December 21, 2005, when he officially became Alex Joseph Anderson. During this time frame and after, Alex quickly bonded to Kelly, so much so, that it seemed at times he may have been surgically attached to her hip. To this day, we laugh about this, because it went on for years – Alex and Kelly were almost inseparable because that is the way Alex wanted it. In retrospect, knowing the bond that was present with his Korean foster mother, I am grateful that he bonded with Kelly so fast.

From early on Aiden and Alex took a liking to each other as well. Of course, there were some rough patches at first, like when Alex would bite Aiden, but as Alex's English vocabulary took off, his tendency to bite his brother subsided. To this day, I would say that although they may not readily admit it, Aiden and Alex are not just brothers but also best friends. As a father, it has been awesome to see the relationship grow and strengthen between these two. It is my hope that they will always maintain the tight bond that all started over bottles of milk on the way home from the airport.

Alex's transition to becoming an Anderson took some time, but, overall, went very well. Shortly after arriving home, he entered speech therapy. Being that Alex was already speaking Korean when we brought him home, one of Kelly's and my chief concerns surrounded his vocabulary and his transition to learning English. Alex's speech therapist was great, and she assured us that the best speech therapy Alex would receive was right at home, via his brothers and his sister. She was correct. Alex's communication with us soon turned from grunts and pointing to understandable words.

As this process played out, we followed up on the questions surrounding Alex's dextrocardia. We proceeded to be put in contact with a Dr. Ralston at Dayton Children's Hospital. Let me start by saying, Dr. Ralston is an awesome pediatric cardiologist! He sat down with us and reviewed Alex's medical history and his medical records and case file that we had obtained from Eastern Social Welfare Society. Dr. Ralston was impressed with the care that was documented in the record, but wanted to run some more testing, as there still were some lingering questions regarding Alex's exact diagnosis. These further tests would prove that Alex was a healthy little boy who would need no further surgeries. Dr. Ralston informed us that his ASD and VSD closures that had been completed in Seoul were top notch. He also informed us that, while Alex's heart was on the right side of his chest, there were no further congenital complications that would need to be addressed through surgery. Remember, Alex's referral had been turned down by over 15 families due to his heart condition. I can only think that God intended for Alex to be an Anderson.

To see how quickly Alex adapted to us as his new family was amazing. It truly showed us the level of resilience this little boy had. Months passed and soon, his Asian looks were the only give away that he had been adopted. Yes, for a long time, he was still a mommy's boy, but it didn't take long for him to start liking me as well. I served as a good fill in when Kelly wasn't around. Alex quickly bonded with his siblings. Breah served as a "mother hen" to him, hovering over both Alex and Aiden, watching their every move. Jay served as a good big brother, alternating between letting Alex (and Aiden) tag along one minute, to teasing, wrestling, and sometimes making them cry the next, like all big brothers do. Months turned into years, and before long, it seemed like Alex had always been with us. The memories of the crying, fighting, puking little Korean boy unwillingly taking a jet ride to America with his new forever family started to fade away. But, one thing always remained in Kelly's and my memory......the love and bond that we saw between Alex and his Korean foster mother.

Throughout the years, Kelly and I have always maintained an openness about adoption with Alex. As anyone who knows us and our family will understand, we keep no secrets from our children. As Alex grew and matured, we would talk about his adoption openly. Kelly is an expert at telling stories, and recited many of these stories to Alex about our travel to Korea and his adoption. One thing Kelly always emphasized to Alex was the care and love that had been given to him by his Korean foster mother for the 18 months prior to us entering his life. For his part, when Alex was younger, he just seemed to like hearing these stories and looking at pictures from our journey in 2005. But, when Alex was about ten years old, he really took an interest in his adoption story and started asking many questions.

Kelly and I had always figured that the day would come when Alex would want to know more about where he had come from. So, when this time arrived, when Alex really started asking questions and inquiring into the process of how the whole adoption occurred, Kelly and I talked and decided that the best way to address his questions was to take him back to Seoul and to visit Eastern Social Welfare Society so that he could see where his journey with us had begun. Like I said, Alex was ten at the time, and we wanted him to be just a little older to ensure that he would always remember a trip like this, so it was decided that we would forgo our "normal" family vacation in the summer of 2015, and would take our children to Seoul, South Korea for a week, just before Alex would turn twelve years old.

CHAPTER 6

REUNITED

Leading up to our return trip to Seoul, we made contact with Children's Home Society of Minnesota, the American adoption agency that we had used for Alex's adoption. This agency provides services for families who have adopted and are wishing to take their children back to visit their home country, so we enlisted their help in setting up a visitation for our family to the Eastern Social Welfare Society in Seoul. Children's Home officials were very accommodating and worked to schedule our visit. As this process played out, one very important question loomed – was there any way they could make contact with and facilitate a visit with Alex's Korean foster mother? We had promised her ten years ago that, if possible, we would return with Alex for a visit, and Kelly and I wanted desperately to make this happen. It was important to us, but we both felt that it was imperative for Alex to meet this woman who loved and cared for him, who spent countless days with him in the hospital, who treated him like he was her own child. As our travel date approached, we were advised that, yes, she was available to meet us at Eastern on June 30th, 2015.

We left on June 28th, 2015, driving to Chicago, then flying to Tokyo, Japan, and finally from there to Seoul, South Korea. While we all looked forward to this trip, I vividly remember that the travel wasn't nearly as exciting as it had been ten years prior, as we eagerly awaited meeting Alex for the first time. Spending over sixteen hours on a jet takes its toll, but finally, we arrived.

Flying into Seoul provides an astounding view of a huge metropolitan area. As we broke through the clouds, we all did anything we could to catch a glimpse out the windows. After touching down and retrieving our luggage, we proceeded through much of the same process as we had years earlier, exchanged US dollars for Korean won, and then entered the commuter rail system that would take us from Incheon International Airport to the apartment we had rented for the week, located in the Hongdae neighborhood of Seoul.

Although it was late by the time we arrived at our apartment, we dropped our luggage off, and headed out to explore. We had just under a week to visit this city, and Alex wanted to squeeze every last second out of it. That first night, seeing the sights, smelling the spices of the food vendors, looking at live squid and octopus in fish tanks along restaurant fronts, just waiting to be made into a fresh meal, and watching the interaction in the markets all made Alex's face glow. I can't imagine, after having so many questions and "not knowing", what it felt like to Alex as he started to experience this, his native country and culture.

While the entire trip to Seoul was something we were all looking forward to, the one item that was circled in everyone's mind was our June 30th visit and tour at Eastern Social Welfare Society and our meeting with Alex's Korean foster mother. Leading up to that day, Alex was filled with questions. Do you think she will be there? What if something happens and she can't make it? Kelly and I could both tell that meeting her was something he wanted to do more than anything, but he worried for some unknown reason that it wouldn't happen.

The day of the meeting, we all were up bright and early and took a family jog around the Hongdae neighborhood, again just taking in the sights, sounds, and culture of Seoul and this particular college neighborhood. We arrived at Eastern about twenty minutes early that day, which for our family is unusual. We were warmly greeted by representatives of the agency and given a tour of the facility and guest house. This tour brought back so many memories for me. I remembered the nursery they have there for the babies that are in the care of the agency. Ten years ago, Breah and my sister Emily had held and rocked those babies for hours on end, with the boys wrapped in blue blankets and the girls wrapped in pink blankets. I remembered the little meeting room with toys down the hallway to the right, where Kelly and I had first met our son and handed him a toy fire truck. The memories seemed so distant, yet were so vivid. As we completed the tour of Eastern, Kelly and I recounted these stories with our children. Alex was very quiet, which is unusual, as he just took it all in.

As the tour of Eastern came to an end, we were advised that we would be taken to a meeting room on the second floor, as Alex's Korean foster mother had arrived. Proceeding up the stairs to this room, we were all quiet with nervous anticipation. This was a moment we had all been looking forward to, hoping that it actually would happen. This was a moment that Alex would always remember, as he finally would meet a woman who had loved him like her own, cared for him day and night, and had been so happy that he found a forever family, yet so sad to see him leave her.

We entered the room, with Alex and the Eastern social worker leading the way. As we turned the corner into the room, there she was sitting on the couch just waiting to see her boy, Seung Joon Ha. Tears of joy immediately flooded her face. Seung Joon and his foster mother were reunited!

The visit lasted about an hour. There wasn't a dry eye in the room at first, but soon, everyone's tears cleared up and laughs, smiles, and hugs flooded the atmosphere of the room. Through the Eastern social worker, who also served as everyone's interpreter, we caught up on the big events of Alex's life that had transpired since that hand off in March of 2005. Kelly and I told his foster mother how good of a boy Alex was, how he did great in school, how he was polite and respectful, how he loved sports, and how he was now a young adolescent that she could be proud of. For her part, Alex's foster mother told Alex over and over again how much she loved him, even to this very day. She held his hand, kissed his face, hugged him, and held his hand some more as he sat by her on the couch. She told Alex of the days that they had spent together in the hospital in Seoul after his surgery. She told Alex about how she had feared first that he might not survive, then, when he had recovered, how she had feared that he might never find a forever family. She talked about how happy she was that Alex now had multiple brothers and sisters. Kelly and I told her about how Aiden and Alex were not only brothers, but best friends as well. She said, "This makes me happy", then proceeded to hug Aiden and Alex at the same time. We took pictures, Alex gave his foster mother a gift that we had brought, then she proceeded to give him a gift that she had purchased for him – a very nice, new backpack – and she related that she hoped this would help him to keep his school items organized. To this day, I don't think there has ever been a book in that backpack, not because of a lack of books, but because this possession is valued to such a high extent by Alex, that he keeps it safely on a shelf in his room so that nothing happens to it. This visit with Alex's foster mother flew by much too fast for us all, but came to an end after about an hour. Kelly and I thanked Alex's foster mother again for being who she was in Alex's life. She thanked us for bringing Alex back to see her. She explained to us that she had been told the same thing many times before by other families, but that this was the first time it had actually happened. She kissed Alex one more time, and gave him one of the tightest hugs I have ever seen, then we all went our separate ways, everyone with a tear in their eye and a smile on their face. This was truly one of the neatest experiences of my entire life, and it was a day I am sure Alex will never forget.

After this meeting took place, it was as if we all could breathe a sigh of relief for Alex. The worry about this meeting actually taking place and all the associated "what ifs" were now in the rear-view mirror. The rest of our trip to Seoul was a great experience. We traveled the city, exploring different areas, neighborhood, markets, and tourist attractions. One day, near the end of our visit, we decided to head to the hospital where Alex's surgery had taken place. Of note, during the time of our travel, there had been a viral MERS (Middle East Respiratory Syndrome) outbreak in Seoul that had started in May and had many of Seoul's inhabitants on edge.

So, with that background, we arrived at Severance Hospital, where Alex's heart surgery had been performed. While Alex had wanted to see this hospital, our other purpose in going there was to try to obtain copies of any medical records that we could, to help piece together information that we didn't have regarding his early months of life. As we walked up to the main entrance of the hospital, we were greeted by red and white signs that stated due to the MERS outbreak, no visitors were being allowed into the hospital. We quickly noticed that everyone entering or exiting the hospital had white masks on their faces covering both their nose and mouth. Seeing this, my response was to say that at least we had been able to see the hospital, but that it looked like we weren't going to be able to go in. Kelly's response was strikingly different.

"I didn't travel halfway across the world to be denied access to Alex's medical records because of some MERS epidemic," Kelly said. Being the medical professional of the family, and understanding the thought process behind the restricted access to the hospital during this time, I tried to explain to Kelly that we just needed to turn around and head out. Needless to say, this was a negotiation that I was not going to win. For anyone who knows Kelly, I think you would agree that when she sets her mind to something, it will get done! And, this case, was no different. Kelly had made up her mind that she was going to do anything possible to obtain Alex's medical file, and that is just what she did.

Kelly and Alex walked into the hospital main entrance, while the rest of us sat on a bench outside and watched. We could see them both as they walked up to a desk, where they paused for a couple minutes. "See, she is not getting in," I said, silently thinking, "I told you so'. But, after a short time of waiting and watching, Jay said, "Dad, look……they are putting on those white masks." I looked up just in time to see Kelly and Alex walking into the main hospital, white masks and all.

Kelly and Alex were in the hospital that day for a little over an hour. As time progressed, the conversation outside turned on me. "Dad, I thought you said there was no way they would let them in," was a common theme. Finally, Kelly and Alex came walking out, with white masks still in place. I noted that Kelly was carrying a file folder with about a two inch thick stack of papers inside. As they discarded the white paper masks into the trash can, the large smiles on their faces were revealed. Alex said, "See dad, mom never gives up. She isn't a quitter!" Kelly, for her part, didn't say much. She just smiled at me, and without her saying a word, I knew what she was thinking….."See, I told you so."

48

I don't know the exact conversations that took place in that hospital in Seoul, South Korea that day. What I do know is that there was one determined mother who would not take no for an answer. Kelly and Alex were admitted to the medical records department of the hospital. When there, they were asked for paperwork identifying Alex and linking him to this boy named Seung Joon Ha. What my wife did was tell the clerk that she was obviously not Alex's birth mother, that we had adopted him in 2005 and changed his name to Alex, that we had an American passport showing this, and that no one in their right mind would travel from America to Seoul in an effort to illegally obtain 10 year old records for a boy who had had open heart surgery in this hospital. I believe Kelly even offered to have Alex take off his shirt to show the scar on his chest. The clerk stopped her, waived in submission, and went and grabbed Alex's file to copy for us. Kelly and Alex found that his heart surgeon had retired a couple years prior and moved south to open his own museum. They also received a copy of every medical record on file for a little boy named Seung Joon Ha, born September 15, 2003, in Busan, South Korea.

A few days later, as we prepared to leave South Korea, we all sat around the table and discussed our trip. Everyone loved getting to see where Alex had come from. Kelly and I enjoyed seeing Alex taking pride in his home country, and, at least to some extent, growing up a little during the trip. Alex talked about how he had to admit, he was ready for some good ole' American food again, but that he had loved it all, especially meeting his foster mother and the backpack she had given him.

CHAPTER 7

A FAMILY
DECISION

Alex's adoption and the subsequent years seeing his growth and integration into our family was a great experience. Kelly, the impetus behind Alex's international adoption, had fulfilled the calling she had felt since high school to adopt. For all my initial reservations, excuses, and reasons for not wanting to adopt, I had not only had a change of heart, but an overhaul of my mentality. My eyes had been opened. I knew Alex's adoption was a calling for our family, it was God's plan. And, though I couldn't quite put my finger on it, I also knew that there was more. Knowing there were so many children in need of a home full of love and stability, it couldn't be so simple as adopting, walking away, and being done, I thought.

Years earlier, in 2004, Kelly and I had looked into becoming foster parents. We had met with a social worker at our local county children services agency and asked many questions about becoming a foster family and how the whole process worked. At that time, remember this was before Alex's adoption, we didn't feel this was the path we wanted to take, because when we initially explored this topic, Kelly and I both just wanted to adopt. I remember sitting at this initial meeting discussing this very thing, the topic of adoption, with the social worker. Kelly and I were informed that the goal of foster care was to reunite children with their birth parents. During this discussion, the social worker very adeptly explained to us the reasons for this goal of the foster care system, and Kelly and I both, at least to some extent, understood the outlook. As we left that meeting, we also both knew that foster care was not the right option for us, which is what spurred us to start exploring international adoption.

Alex needed time to be the baby of our family, but as he grew older, I started to wrestle with the question of what more could we do? My thoughts drifted back to that 2004 meeting and our exploration of becoming a foster family. While it wasn't the right path to take way back then, I started to get the feeling that it may be the right path to take for our family now. Kelly, for her part, dealt with some of the same feelings. She had seen the need that was out there, the children needing families to love them, and her mind constantly raced, asking questions of how could she further impact the lives of children.

The questions that both of us were asking ourselves spurred numerous conversations. We discussed the option of adopting internationally again, however, we quickly determined that financially, we couldn't afford it. After all, we were still paying off the loan that was taken for Alex's adoption. As this discussion went further, we both circled back to the option of becoming a foster family. Our outlook and goals were different now. We both agreed that we weren't intent on adopting, like we had been years ago, but that rather, we just wanted to find a way to make a difference in the life of a child. Now, becoming a foster family seemed like the right path to take.

Feeling this calling, Kelly and I also realized that it couldn't be just an "us" decision. This needed to be something that was discussed as a family, and it was something that our children had to be on board with as well. So, in early 2012, we had a family meeting to broach this topic. At the time, Breah was 13, Jay was 11, Aiden was 9, and Alex was 8 years old. As the meeting came to order, I remember them all looking at Kelly and I with puzzled looks.....like they were wondering what bad news we were about to break. We discussed our desire to take the necessary classes that were required to become a foster family. We discussed that as a foster family, we may never adopt again – that wasn't our goal – but that we, as a family, would hopefully have the opportunity to make a difference in the lives of other children. Our kids asked questions, and we answered them to the best of our ability. In the end, everyone was on board. This idea of becoming a foster family was the path that we all agreed to travel.

In the months that followed, Kelly and I signed up to take the required 36 hours of training to become State Certified foster parents. After discussion, we decided to pursue obtaining our foster license from a neighboring county rather than our home county. That fact may seem strange, but it is the path we took. We had our own reasons for proceeding in this direction – mainly due to thoughts that we would be more likely to get a foster placement because it was a much larger county and agency – but in retrospect, I am confident that we took this path because it was God's plan, even if we didn't realize it at the time.

Our classes to become certified foster parents consisted of a varied schedule. Some classes were held for 3 hours in the evening on week nights, others were held for 6 hours on Saturdays. One constant through all of our classes, however, was our trainer Maggie Lupton. Maggie directed and taught most of our initial certification class, and through our initial class and in ensuing years has become a mentor and friend to Kelly and me. I can say without a doubt, her honest and direct approach at training us as foster parents has helped contribute to the focus and mentality that Kelly and I have carried on as foster parents, the idea that above all we are advocates for the children entrusted to our care, that we treat all children no differently than we treat our own children, and that we fight for what is right for all children, just as we would our own children, both biological and adopted, because in our family, there is no difference.

The decision to become foster parents, and therefore a foster family, had been a group decision. That being the case, each time we would complete a section of our initial training course, we would go home and have a pseudo family training session. Kelly and I would both review what we had learned in class, discuss it with Breah, Jay, Aiden, and Alex, and answer any questions that they may have with regard to these items. Quite honestly, it became very evident that our kids looked forward to us having class because of these discussions. They were "all in" on being a foster family. We had made it very clear to them that this was a group effort, that we all had a role to play, and they relished their part in this endeavor. Our family training sessions served to pass on this education we were receiving to all the members of our team/family. Additionally, holding these discussions with our children and answering the questions that resulted from them, served to de-mystify this whole process of becoming a foster family.

Kelly and I completed our training in the fall of 2012, and were certified as State approved foster parents on November 30, 2012. Upon certification, we both nervously awaited a phone call asking us to be foster parents for a child. While we were confident this was the next step in God's plan for our family, it was hard not knowing when the call would come. We waited throughout the month of December and had no calls. It didn't take long and Kelly became worried that we wouldn't get a call, which, now is very funny when we think about it. I remember Kelly asking me, "Do you think they don't like us?" I would reply that I wasn't concerned, that I was sure that they liked us and realized that we would be a good foster family. Kelly would then follow up that question with, "Well, why do you think they haven't called us yet?" I distinctly remember once answering her, "Because they like me, but don't like you." Needless to say, she did not like my attempt at humor.

Our wait for a call lasted through December, and extended into January, then February of 2013. As weeks passed by, Kelly became increasingly concerned that we were not going to get a call. I would say that this worry was not born out of not trusting God's plan for our lives, but rather, it came from wanting so much to touch and make a difference in a child's life. That desire has always burned brightly in my wife's heart, and as we waited and waited for a call, it was almost as if she couldn't contain it.

Finally, on February 8, 2013, I received a phone call from Kelly informing me that "we had gotten called." The agency had talked with her asking if we would be interested in the placement of a little boy the following week, as a sort of respite type placement for a family member who had been caring for him. Kelly, of course, gathered the information and said "yes". Our journey as foster parents would begin the following week, on Monday February 11, 2013, when Joel would arrive at our home.

CHAPTER 8

RAPID EXPANSION

My first memory of Joel is when this chubby, curly haired little boy arrived at our home. As he walked up to our door, he flattened his nose against the window, peering in. Joel came into our home this first time, and Kelly and I didn't know what to expect. We had been told that he was a handful, that there were concerns that he may be showing signs of autism. At this first introduction, we were informed by his case worker of how Joel had pulled a Houdini and escaped from his car seat on the way to our home. We were further informed about concerns relating to Joel's development. He was behind the curve. He didn't speak well, saying only a couple words. He was hard to understand. We were told there were many challenges that seemed to lay ahead for Joel, but Kelly and I didn't care. All we wanted to do was love this little boy and try to make him feel as safe and secure as possible.

Over the coming weeks, as we found out more and more about Joel's background, we started to realize why Joel was such a handful at times. Joel, who was 3 1/2 years old when he came to us, had lived in about 13 different homes prior to arriving at ours. He had been hospitalized after falling out a second story window. He had been found playing in parks by himself in the middle of the night. He had been abused and neglected. He had lived with numerous friends and family members. He had had a very tumultuous first couple years.

As I noted, Joel could not communicate well. The first couple weeks were a learning experience for our family as we tried to learn and understand what he was saying. As days turned into weeks, we also started noticing other behaviors with Joel. He would bang his head, he would chew on his nails, his clothes, his toys, and he would become frustrated easily. As these behaviors became evident, we searched for help and answers for Joel. He was enrolled in speech and occupational therapy soon after arriving in our home. Just before coming to our home, he had also been taken to an ENT, where it was found that he had a small bead embedded in his ear. After this was removed, the head banging stopped. Joel had his huge, swollen tonsils and adenoids taken out. He felt better, and he looked better. And, as all this started to take place, he became more comfortable in our home, and very quickly became a "mommy's boy". The bond that Joel quickly started forming with Kelly was nothing short of amazing. Here he was, at 3 1/2, with a woman whom he had only known for weeks, and he was thriving under her care. That being said, I don't want to diminish the contributions of our whole family to this initial introduction and acclimation of Joel, but anyone in our family would tell you, he immediately and amazingly started bonding and attaching to Kelly.

It really is amazing the difference that love and stability can make in the life of a child. Things that many of us take for granted such as sleeping in the same bed every night, knowing that there will be breakfast when you wake up in the morning, feeling the embrace of open arms and a tight hug before going to bed make children feel safe, secure, and stable. These things, and many more, are what Kelly excels in. She just has a knack at being a mom and knowing what a child needs and when they need it. Shortly after Joel moved in with us, Kelly applied these skills and started being able to read him like a book. When she sensed his frustrations, she would comfort him. She knew when he just needed held and rocked in the chair. Just as much as Joel's speech and occupational therapists worked with Joel at his appointments, Kelly worked with him at home. It truly was amazing to see it all unfold. You literally could sense the relief in Joel's demeanor when he was in Kelly's arms.

As this unfolded, Kelly and I talked about how much we loved having Joel in our home. Even though at times it was hard, we truly felt that we were doing what God had intended for us to do at this point in our lives. Additionally, we also saw the impact it was having on Breah, Jay, Aiden, and Alex. They all had taken to Joel, each in their own way. Whether it was Breah helping Joel to get ready for bed, or Jay playing "trucks" with him, or even Aiden and Alex throwing any and all types of balls with him, they all were playing a part in Joel's growing acceptance of and attachment to our family.

During the next couple months, Kelly and I received a call for a short term foster placement of a little boy. After this short term placement, we also provided respite care on a couple occasions for a young teenage girl. The early worries of "are they even going to call us" turned into the eager anticipation of "when is the next call going to come?"

That next call did come at the most unexpected time. On May 4, 2013, in the early morning hours, Kelly received the call. I was working my shift at the fire department. We had had a house fire that night. Shortly after coming back from that call and cleaning everything up, we had received another emergency call for an ambulance run. I vividly remember that early morning about 3 am. It was my birthday, I had been out most of the night, I had not yet slept, and all I wanted to do was finish my shift so I could go home and rest. We were returning from the hospital in the ambulance when my cell phone rang. It was Kelly on the other end of the line.

"Brian, I just got a call asking if I could go to a police department and pick up a sibling group", Kelly stated. Wow, that was unexpected, so I thoughtfully replied, "OK". After a couple seconds of silence, Kelly asked me, "So, what do you want me to do?" "What would Jesus do? Go get them", I said. And with that, our lives were about to change again.

This seems like a good time to remind everyone of a couple things. Years back, Kelly had always talked about fostering and adopting. Initially, I had thought of every excuse in the book to not do that. I had brought up every worst case scenario I could think of to try to dissuade Kelly from forcing me to be a part of this vision she had for our family. But God had a different plan. Here we were, years later, with an unexpected call at 3 am asking us to pick up a sibling group, and without even hesitating, when Kelly asked me what I thought, I said, "Go get them." I had lost sight of what I wanted our family to be, and, with the help of Kelly's vision, prayers, and persistence, had taken hold of what God wanted our family to be. This is a lesson that I have learned very well though our family's formation and experiences – that holding onto what we want, no matter what it is, only holds us back. It is only through letting go, and letting God guide and direct our paths that we find the plan and purpose that He has for us. And is it only in following His plan and purpose for our lives that we find true happiness and contentment. Now back to the story......

After our short phone conversation that night, Kelly headed out of town to go to pick up the sibling group that we would come to know as Kate and Trey. Kate, who was 5 years old at the time, and Trey, who was 3, had been in foster care for about a year prior to Kelly and I receiving the call. The reason that we received the call that night was due to a domestic violence incident that the police had become involved in that evening. It was not the first domestic incident that had occurred at the home, but it was the first time that arrests were being made. When the police asked about family members or grandparents who could be called to pick up Kate and Trey, they finally found out that Kate and Trey were foster children who were in the care of these folks. Kate and Trey were immediately removed and taken to the local police department, which is what generated the call that Kelly received.

As Kelly entered the police department that night, she was lead back to a small room where Kate and Trey were sitting. Upon entering the room, Kate looked up with her big brown eyes, and upon seeing Kelly for the first time said, "Wow, you look like a nice mom!" She could not have been more correct with that first assessment of the situation.

On the ride home that early morning, Kate talked and talked and talked. She seemed happy to have a "nice mom" who would listen to her and hold a conversation. Trey, on the other hand, just whined and grunted despite Kelly trying to strike up a conversation with him as well. As Kelly came back into our home town, sensing that both Kate and Trey were hungry, she asked them if they wanted to go on a late night snack run. They both said "yes", so the expedition inside of Walmart early that morning began. The rules of the expedition were that Kate and Trey could grab anything that sounded good to them. By the time it was over, they headed out of Walmart with bags full of milk, juice, chips, ice cream, donuts, and other assorted snacks.

I arrived home that morning from my shift at the fire department tired and ready for some sleep, but I was excited to meet Kate and Trey for the first time. As I walked into the house, I found a quiet living room, with Kate and Trey both fast asleep on the couch. The kitchen was full of empty bags of donuts along with various other partially eaten snacks. As I looked down at Kelly, who was fast asleep in a recliner, and at Kate and Trey on the couch, I thanked God for these two little children and prayed that He would help Kelly and I fill the role in their lives they needed us to fill, whatever that may be.

CHAPTER 9

FULL CIRCLE

Kate and Trey acclimated to our family in much different ways. Kate, from day one, was a trusting, caring, loving little girl who immediately looked at us as her family. Trey, on the other hand, took some time to start warming up to all of us. He had a very cold attitude toward Kelly and me at first, which is very understandable. Kate and Trey had been in the foster care system for over a year. As we would come to find out, they had been placed with foster parents who mistreated and neglected them. These same foster parents, as I said earlier, had a history of domestic issues, all of which Kate and Trey were witnesses to. As all of this information came to light, Kate and Trey's case worker seemed shocked. We had been advised that Kate and Trey's former foster parents were in the closing stages of finalizing the needed paperwork and process to adopt them. Thankfully, they were rescued from this situation before that had happened!

Much like when Joel had come into our home, Kate and Trey experienced very quickly what a mother's love was like. All of our family played a role in helping them get used to their new surroundings and family dynamics, but Kelly's nurturing, motherly instincts were, at least initially, what they both needed the most. As I have said before, stability and demonstrated love and affection prove invaluable to children who have experienced trauma, and Kelly is an expert at handing this out.

After Kate and Trey's initial placement, the summer of 2013 seemed to come very quickly. Our family had experienced a rapid expansion going from 4 to 7 children in a matter of months. The summer that year was a time of all of us learning about each other and learning how to be a family. That may sound strange, but it really was a learning experience. Our older children had to adjust to having a "group" of younger children in the home. While Breah, Jay, Aiden, and Alex all did great in helping Kate, Trey, and Joel whenever needed, they also had to learn that there wasn't quite as much of mom and dad to go around as there used to be. Kate, Trey, and Joel had to learn what it was like to live in our home. They had to learn who new grandparents, aunts, uncles, and cousins were. They had to learn to live with new brothers and sisters. I am not going to lie, it wasn't always easy, but it was worth every second.

As we moved through the summer and into the back to school time of year, it seemed that things settled down a bit, and our family started to settle into a groove, so to speak. Kate, Trey, and Joel all entered pre-school, and as time progressed, their standing as current foster children as well as where their cases were heading started to take shape.

As I previously said, Kate and Trey weren't all that far away from being adopted by their previous foster parents prior to coming to our home, therefore Kelly and I knew it was a distinct possibility that we may have the chance to adopt them. At that point, it really hadn't been discussed with their case worker, but we knew if it became an option, we would absolutely welcome them becoming a permanent part of our family. During this time, Kelly and I had noted that frequently Kate would wake up in the middle of the night and come walking into our room. We would wake up when we heard her walk in, and one of us would get up with her, give her a hug, and tuck her back into her bed. After this had gone on for some time, Kelly asked Kate why she was doing this – coming into our room at night. Kate replied, "Because I just want to make sure you are here." That simple statement she made said a lot to us.

A couple days after Kate had explained that to Kelly, again, we both woke up one night hearing the creaking of our bedroom floor. Initially, I didn't say anything, but we both watched as Kate walked to my side of the bed. I sat up in bed and said, "Kate, you don't have anything to worry about. We are both here." Kate just stood by the side of our bed with tears in her eyes. I asked her what was wrong. Kate replied, "I like it here with you and mom. Do I ever have to leave?" I answered that question with the only appropriate answer available saying, "No Kate, you never have to leave our home."

That night, after tucking Kate back into her bed, Kelly asked me how I could say that to her. We thought we knew how things might progress with Kate and Trey, but, we also knew there were no guarantees. I understood this fact, but I just had this feeling inside telling me that all the children in our home had been placed there for a reason – because they needed a forever family. I related this to Kelly. I couldn't explain it, but I just had a peace about it. That night, lying in bed after our visit from Kate, we talked about the possibility of our family permanently expanding to 7 children. It was not by any means what we had envisioned or expected when we decided to become a foster family, but we both felt very confident that, if this was God's plan for our family, then we were willing to follow that call.

It is at this point, I would like to reminisce a little. This willingness to follow God's plan for our family was a complete change of heart for me. Remember, I was the one who had years ago thought adoption was a neat thing – for others to pursue. I was the one who only wanted to talk about why we couldn't adopt. I was the one who, at every discussion, attempted to place roadblocks in the path to adopting and expanding our family. At that time, I was the one who was running away from God's call.

This may seem to be a simplistic way of looking at things. Some would say that I just was afraid of the unknown. However, I can tell you that is not the case. Even through all those discussions Kelly and I had had years earlier, I felt it. I knew that Kelly was right and I felt the calling to follow her lead, but I had intentionally tried to shove it aside. I knowingly had tried to set my own course, a course different than what I knew deep down was the course that God wanted us to travel. To this day, I am thankful for Kelly's persistence and that God grabbed my attention and changed my heart, mind, and attitude toward adoption. To me, this night in my life represents the time where I had totally bought in to God's plan for our family. I had come full circle. I think of how different things might have been had this not happened, and, to be quite honest, it almost makes me sick to think that because of my own stubbornness and unwillingness to hear God's call, what effect this may have had on others.

I think this presents a lesson that I hope can be taken away from our story. Listen to that quiet voice inside. Hear God's calling for your life. He has a plan for us all. Sometimes His plans will make you uncomfortable. Sometimes His plans are not what you may have envisioned. But, I can tell you, there is always a purpose to His plan for your life. Sometimes that purpose is hard to see. But, in the end, His plan is always perfect. Through following His plan, things that you would have never imagined can and will happen. Have faith, because when you follow God's plan for your life, He is always right there beside you......even when you can't see it.

"For I know the plans I have for you," declares the Lord, "plans to prosper you and not to harm you, plans to give you hope and a future." Jeremiah 29:11

CHAPTER 10

PERMANENCY

Permanency. Such a simple word, but such a complex idea. Permanency can be described as or likened to durability, lastingness, enduringness, and strength.

In early 2014, after almost nine months in our home, permanency became the topic of discussion as it related to both Kate and Trey. Permanency was being sought for both of them, and Kelly and I were asked if we were interested in becoming the permanent parents for both through adoption. Eagerly, we both said, "Yes."

Through this process, we were very open and honest with both Kate and Trey, who were ages six and four at the time. As best we could, we explained what permanency would mean for both of them – that we would become their mom and dad forever, that our family would become their forever family, that they would always have a place to call home, and that their names would change officially making them Andersons. It was evident, as much as we wanted them to become an official part of our family, they wanted to achieve this permanency as well.

All the required paperwork was filled out and signed. An adoption date was scheduled for March of 2014. And, as we waited for Kate and Trey's adoption date to come, permanency also started to become a topic of discussion for Joel.

As much as Kate and Trey needed permanency in their lives, Joel needed it just as well. Remember, Joel had lived in a multitude of different homes prior to being placed with our family, and he experienced numerous developmental issues, a lot of which stemmed from the lack of stability present over his first three years of life. Shortly after being placed in our home, Joel had quickly bonded to all of us, but mostly Kelly. Wait a second.....let me rephrase that. Joel had quickly bonded to Kelly, so by extension he had bonded with all of us. So, as we moved towards the adoption date for Kate and Trey, permanency options were being discussed for Joel. Of course, when asked if we were willing to become the permanent parents for Joel through adoption, Kelly and I again eagerly responded, "Yes."

The weeks and days leading up to Kate and Trey's adoption were filled with excitement on all parts. Kelly and I were excited to finalize the adoption. Breah, Jay, Aiden, and Alex were excited to officially welcome a new brother and sister to the family. Kate and Trey were excited that this would mean they never had to leave. They talked about it constantly. As adoption became the buzz word around the house and as discussions continued behind the scenes related to Joel's permanency, Joel asked if he could be adopted too. He understood the upcoming day was Kate and Trey's adoption date, but asked when his would be. Kelly and I assured Joel that we were hoping to adopt him as well, but that we just didn't know for sure when it would take place, which was obviously not the answer any of us wanted to give. However, just a short time before Kate and Trey's adoption day, the paperwork for Joel was completed. After being asked by the agency if we wanted to adopt Joel, Kelly and I made it official, attesting to our intent to pursue his adoption.

Kate and Trey officially became Anderson children on March 14, 2014, in the Allen County Probate Court in Lima, Ohio. It was a great day, filled with many smiles, camera flashes, and topped off with pizza and bowling. Kate and Trey had permanently joined our family. There was no going back, and the comfort of that seemed to wash over them that night as Kelly and I tucked them in bed, becoming very evident when Trey said, "I am Trey Anderson now, right mom and dad?", a big smile stretching across his small face.

The following weeks were met with more anticipation, as we all waited for the notification period to end with regard to our intent to adopt Joel. As we had signified our intent to adopt when asked by the Agency, there was a 30 day time period where all known relatives had to be notified that Joel would be placed for adoption if no relatives stepped forward to request placement. This, of course, was a somewhat stressful time, however, Joel was now going on five years old and had been in our home for almost a year and a half. While we worried about the "what if", we also felt a peace that Joel was right where he belonged.

In late March, Kelly and I took Joel to Nationwide Children's Hospital in Columbus for an appointment with one of his physicians. During this visit, we received an email from one of Joel's caseworkers at Allen County Children Services requesting that we call them to set up a meeting at our earliest convenience.

This seemed strange to both Kelly and me, so, from the doctor's office in Columbus that day, we called the agency to see what was needed. We were advised that they needed to talk to us and that they wanted it to be a face to face meeting. As we would be traveling past Lima on our way home from Columbus that day, we advised the agency that we could stop in to meet later that afternoon.

Driving home that day, we were both very quiet. Neither of us knew why this sudden meeting was necessary, however both of us had our concerns, worries, and fears. As we arrived at the agency in Lima, walking in, I looked over and saw Joel clinging to Kelly, squeezing her tightly around the neck. My mind raced, thinking of the worst case scenario of why this meeting would be called so suddenly. I looked at Joel draped around this woman, his foster mother, the woman to whom he had bonded so quickly and so strongly, and I thought to myself, "There is no way they would ever take him away from her, away from the safety and stability that he has come to know and flourish in."

Kelly, Joel, and I were led into the agency to a meeting room. Someone tried to distract Joel and take him into a separate room to play with some toys so that Kelly and I could attend the meeting alone. Joel would not have it. He clung to Kelly, so toys were brought into the meeting room, yet, Joel just wanted to sit on Kelly's lap. In the room were Joel's case worker, and two other agency officials, Brad Rabley and Michelle Voorhees. The news they were about to tell us was not what Kelly and I wanted to hear.

"Be still and know that I am God." Psalm 46:10

CHAPTER 11

FAITH

For Kelly and me, the meeting that day was filled with shock, worry, and tears. We were told that after our notice of intent to adopt was sent out, a relative of Joel's had stepped forward wanting placement of Joel. Keep in mind, Joel was now going on five years old and had been in our home for over a year. During this time, Joel had had visitation with some of his family. These family members who had visited with Joel had come to realize that Joel was doing well, and had expressed to Kelly and me that Joel was exactly where he needed to be. That being the case, the family member who was now intent on taking placement of Joel was a relative whom Joel would not even know or recognize. It was a relative who had not visited Joel while he was in foster care; a relative who had literally not seen Joel in years. Even with that being the case, the agency officials told Kelly and I that they were going to start visits between Joel and this relative the following week and that they were going to pursue placement of Joel with his relative.

Kelly and I, of course, protested. At the meeting, we raised numerous concerns with this decision. We asked where had this relative been all these years? If they wanted placement of Joel, why hadn't they even so much as visited him over the time Joel had lived with us? We were assured that while all these questions were understood by agency officials, as foster parents, we weren't entitled to answers. We left this meeting feeling sick, and Joel, while he wasn't sure what was going on, knew something was wrong.

Over the next couple days, we had numerous additional phone conversations with agency officials. During these conversations, again, we were told that as foster parents, we weren't entitled to answers to our questions. Even though we had cared for Joel every day for over a year, and even though the family members who had maintained contact and visitation with Joel during that time were happy that we were planning to adopt him, the fact remained that someone who was related by blood had decided that they wanted placement, so, to the Agency, we were now just caretakers until that placement could be arranged.

As I had said, visits for Joel with this relative were already being scheduled for the following week, so, with nowhere else to turn, Kelly and I took two actions. For the first time in either of our lives, we obtained our own legal representation, Jerry Johnson, who was the attorney who had done Kate and Trey's adoptive finalization. Sitting in Jerry's office, we explained the events of the last couple days, our concerns, our unanswered questions, and our worry about the potential effects this proposed placement may have on Joel. Jerry was shocked by the turn of events and assured us he would absolutely represent us and start digging into the circumstances surrounding Joel's case.

Secondly, Kelly made an impassioned phone call and plea to one of the directors at the children services agency. To this day, I am still not sure what was all discussed, questioned, or said during that phone call, but whatever it was, it raised enough concern that the pending first visit with this relative scheduled for the following week was postponed pending completion of a background check and home study of this individual.

Our family moved forward with Joel and with our lives. All of us were affected by what we knew was going on behind the scenes. We had questions, concerns, and worries, not knowing what the future was going to bring for Joel. As hard as it was, we did our best to keep faith that God was in control. Personally, this was a struggle for me. I asked many questions of God during this time. And every time I started to question things, I just kept hearing that still small voice repeatedly answer, "I love Joel more than you", which served to remind me that God was still in control.

Behind the scenes, things continued to happen and God continued to work. We received anonymous information that there were relatives of Joel who actually worked at the Agency. At first, we didn't believe it, but we came to find out it was, in fact, true. Jerry, our attorney, continued to ask questions and make phone calls. We received notification that, due to our concerns regarding the agency's ability to show "impartiality", knowing relatives of Joel worked there, the background check and home study of Joel's relative wanting placement would be done by a children services agency from a different Ohio county. For weeks, we heard almost nothing more. But in May, we received a phone call. We were advised that the background check had revealed concerns and the home study application of Joel's relative had been found to contain lies, so the home study had been failed. Our adoption of Joel would be allowed to proceed!

Joel's adoption was scheduled for June of 2014. To try to sum up what my feelings were as we moved towards this finalization date is somewhat difficult. First and foremost, I was thankful. My faith had definitely wavered, but God had proven that He was in control of Joel's future. I was also mad, frustrated, displeased, upset, happy, and relieved all at the same time. I was mad that Joel and our family had been put through this period of stress. From the beginning, Kelly and I had made very well known that what was being lost on the decision makers was multiple references in the Ohio Revised Code that state, in all cases, the best interests of the child shall be served. Additionally, for children who had been taken into permanent custody, like Joel, the Ohio Administrative Code clearly states, "an adoptive placement shall be considered the least restrictive setting" (OAC 5101:2-42-05-G). I was frustrated with the system that too easily loses sight of this. I was displeased that, as long term foster parents, we had been told that we were not entitled to answers for the very appropriate questions we had asked. I was upset to think that if we had just laid down and not stood for what we believed was in Joel's best interests, who knows where he would have ended up being placed. But yet, I was happy and relieved that we would be able to adopt Joel, that he would become our son, an Anderson.

Feeling these surges of emotions, I couldn't help but think back to that still, small voice I had repeatedly heard saying, "I love Joel more than you do." How true that proved to be. Despite all the worry and fear, God had a plan for Joel, and that plan was for him to be adopted into our family. On June 26, 2014, in the Allen County Probate Court in Lima, Ohio, Joel became a part of our forever family.

"Faith takes God without any 'if's." **D.L.Moody**

CHAPTER 12

AN OLD MAN

Our family had grown. Kelly and I were now the proud parents of seven children. We were thankful and felt very blessed. We were also done…..done as foster parents and done adopting. In the weeks leading up to and immediately following Joel's adoption, we had discussed this at length. Both of us, without any shred of doubt, had decided that we were not going to take any more foster placements and that in a few months, when our family's foster license was set to expire, we were not going to renew it. Many things had pointed us in that direction, but the circumstances leading up to and surrounding Joel's adoption had cemented us on that fact. Our house was full, our time was stretched between seven children, and we were not going to risk subjecting our family to another situation like what we had just experienced.

The month following Joel's adoption was a great time for our family. For the first time ever, as the Anderson family of nine, we took a family vacation to Florida. It was truly a time of relaxation and fun for us all, as we got to see the looks on Kate, Trey, and Joel's faces when they saw the ocean in person for the first time in their lives. We returned from vacation that summer looking forward to annual home town activities that were set to begin in late July. One of these activities included a 5K run during the Celina Lake Festival. Leading up to this run, our church, Grand Lake United Methodist, had started a running group – as part of the Team 413 Gracerunner Ministries – that was training together for the Lake Festival 5K run. Kelly and a couple of the kids had joined in the training with this group to run the 5K, and the evening before the Lake Festival started that summer, Kelly had been asked to help at a booth selling t-shirts promoting Team 413 and the running team. This was the evening that Kelly met an old man......

Working the booth that evening, Kelly had Breah with her. I was at home with the other kids. Toward the end of the evening, Kelly was approached by an old man. This man, as Kelly recounts, had a long, scraggly beard and a worn, haggard look to him. He was wearing a pair of dirty bib overalls. Kelly remembers that her first impression as this man approached was that she thought he looked like he may have been either a little disoriented or intoxicated. This old man approached the booth, and Kelly greeted him by saying, "Hi, how are you?" As he started to reply, from his body odor, it was evident to Kelly that he had not showered in some time. The old man kindly, but oddly, replied by asking Kelly, "How many kids do you have?" Kelly responded that she had seven children. Immediately, without missing a beat, this old man replied matter of factly, "Well, you are about to have eight." Kelly laughed, and related to this man that she was fine with seven and that would be as many as she would have. This old man was persistent in claiming that he was right. He proceeded to informed Kelly, "Nope, a beautiful baby girl with dark hair and dark eyes is coming your way." Kelly told the man that we had both biological children and adopted children, which is how we got to seven kids, but informed him that he was wrong because we had already advised the agency that we were with that we were done taking placements. Therefore, as Kelly told this man, "We really are done having any more children."

In most cases, you would think that this conversation would have ended. But, as Kelly recounts, this man continued, almost to the point of being annoying. "I'm just telling you, a little girl is coming your way," he said. Kelly, chuckling, asked him, "What makes you say that?" "I just know things," he replied. At this point, Kelly couldn't believe that she was still having this conversation with a stranger she didn't even know. She turned to Breah, who had been standing behind her, giving Breah the "what in the world is going on here?" look. Just seconds later, Kelly turned back around to see if this gentleman had any more to tell her, but when she turned he was already walking away from the booth. Breah said to Kelly, "Mom, why would he say that? That was so weird!" As Breah started to question the events that had just transpired, something stirred inside of Kelly. Could this guy have known we were adoptive parents? If so, is there any chance he could have known our kids or maybe the birth parents or a family member of one of our kids? Was it possible a family member may ask us to take a sibling or a relative of one of our kids?

Kelly's mind started to race. This was one of the strangest conversations she had ever been a part of, and she had to know the reasoning behind it. She turned and looked at Breah, telling her, "Stay here and man the booth" as Kelly headed out to track down this old man that had walked off literally less than 30 seconds earlier. Kelly headed off following the direct path that she saw this gentleman walking. At the time, it was not too crowded, so Kelly was sure she would be able to spot this old man in his overalls. However, as Kelly searched and scanned everyone around that day, she found no trace of the man that she had just talked to.

After searching for some time, Kelly determined that he was not going to be found, so she gave me a call and recounted this peculiar story to me. I vividly remember my response at the end of her story. Laughing, I said to Kelly, "Well, he must have been drunk, because if he only knew what we had just been through with Joel's adoption, he would also know that he was absolutely wrong in his assessment of how many children we would have!"

That day was July 24th, 2014.........a day none of us will ever forget. And, had we known then what we know now, we would have paid a little more attention to the focus of and the Bible verse behind Team 413 Gracerunner Minitries:

"The likelihood of you doing something extraordinary in your life without significant sacrifice is impossible. God will give you the strength but YOU must supply the effort! Keep plugging away – the impossible will become a reality when HIS strength and YOUR effort collide."

Chris A. Gillespie, Team 413 Gracerunner Ministries, www.team413.org

"For I can do everything through Christ, who gives me strength." Philippians 4:13

CHAPTER 13

DARK HAIR AND DARK EYES

Thursday August 7th, 2014, started out as a normal day in the Anderson household. Just a couple weeks before school would start, the kids were enjoying what remained of their summer. Kelly was busy with her normal "mom" routine, keeping the house in order, checking to make sure all needed school supplies had been found or purchased and checked off each child's list, and making sure, in general, all things were taken care of at home. I had to work that day, so I was in Bluffton, Ohio, working my weekly 24 hour shift at Life Flight. Breah was busy with high school soccer and had a game in Findlay, Ohio, that evening. It was just another day in the life of our large family.

That evening, while at work, my phone rang. Looking at the screen, I saw that it was Kelly calling me. I hated when my work schedule conflicted with any of the kids' school and sports events, so I always asked Kelly to give me updates when I was working. With that being the case, I figured Kelly was calling to give me an update on Breah's game. Then I noticed the time. It was just a little after 6 p.m., which meant that Breah's game hadn't even started yet.

Answering the phone, I asked Kelly how things were going and, without giving her a chance to answer, I also asked if she was on her way to Breah's game yet. "Brian, I haven't even left for Breah's game. I am calling you because we need to talk," Kelly said. That was definitely not the answer I was expecting, and it was absolutely an answer that immediately put me on high alert.

"I received a phone call a while ago from Allen County Children Services asking if we would take a placement," Kelly informed me. "Well, obviously you told them "no", right? I mean, we have talked about this," was my response. Kelly confirmed that she had, in fact, told them no. But, as she went on, Kelly proceeded to tell me that after that initial phone call and denial, she received a second phone call. It was this second phone call from the agency that was the genesis of the current phone conversation Kelly and I were having.

Kelly informed me that the agency was requesting us to take a short term placement of a child. The agency had told Kelly that it would probably be only a two to four day placement as there was a relative from out of state that had been advised of the situation and would be coming to pick up this child early the following week. With this information in hand, Kelly was calling me to see what I thought, and to, as a team, make a decision.

I was very hesitant. As thoughts started to swirl, I told myself, we already have our hands full enough. I repeated this thought out loud to Kelly. "I know," Kelly said. "That is why I didn't commit to anything and why I told them I needed to talk with you." As I started to feel more confident in this "hands full enough" concept, Kelly asked me if I wanted to know the rest of the information that she had been given. "Of course," I replied. As Kelly filled me in, I came to understand that this proposed short term placement would be for a thirteen day old baby girl. Baby girl.....Breah, now 16 years old, was a "baby girl" once, but that had been a long time ago. We had not even known Kate, now six years old, when she was a "baby girl". Baby girl.....my mind raced. "Wouldn't it be fun to have a little baby girl to hold and rock to sleep for a couple days?" I asked myself. Soon, I found myself repeating this question to Kelly.

We talked for a short while longer discussing pros and cons. After all, we no longer had a baby car seat. We didn't have a baby bassinet. We did still have a crib, however that was in the attic and would need reassembled. But, we couldn't get away from the thought of how much we would enjoy taking care of a baby again, especially because we knew it was just going to be for a couple days. For me, the "hands full enough" concept that had been developed just a short time ago, started to crumble. For Kelly, I think that she never bought into this concept to begin with. She just knew that she had to follow along with me until I started to see things her way (she knows how to play me like that).

As our phone conversation concluded, we decided that we would accept this short term placement. Kelly needed to head to the agency to pick up this little girl, so I told Kelly that I would text Breah's phone, letting her know why her mother wouldn't be at her soccer game. Suddenly, the 15 or so hours that remained in my shift seemed like forever. I couldn't wait to get home and meet this little one.

Arriving at the agency that evening, Kelly walked in not knowing what to expect. What greeted her was an absolutely beautiful little thirteen day old baby girl. As the light of this situation started to dawn on Kelly, chills spread throughout her body. You see, despite Kelly's initial turning down of this placement, despite the second phone call and subsequent conversation where I tried to turn down this placement, despite both Kelly and me and our decision that we were absolutely done taking placements, Kelly was picking up a little girl named Madeline. She just happened to have a ton of dark brown hair, and big, beautiful dark brown eyes.

As the evening dragged on at work, I eagerly anticipated Kelly's phone call to update me on the situation. This phone call came later that evening as Kelly was on her way home. She filled me in on the small amount of information we had been given. Kelly told me that the case worker had reiterated to her that a relative had been contacted and the expectation was that this relative would be picking Madeline up early next week. She filled me in on the handful of supplies I needed to pick up when I came home from work the following morning. Then, she filled me in on the rest of the story, so to speak. "Brian," she said, "Do you remember that old guy I talked to out by the lake a couple weeks ago?" "Yes," I said, "it's kind of weird now, right? Especially, because we got this short term placement of a baby girl." Kelly agreed, but told me there was more to the story. "I just want to make sure you realize a couple additional things," Kelly told me. "Number one, Madeline has dark brown hair and big dark brown eyes." "Ok, that just makes what he said more weird," I replied. What Kelly said to me next, at least initially, didn't really make me any difference. But Kelly had already connected the dots. "Number two, Madeline is fourteen days old." "I thought they said she was thirteen days old," I replied. "But, what difference does that make anyway?" "Think about it," Kelly said. She was playing a game with me now. Think about it.....think about it. I just didn't get what she was talking about. In fact, I thought this little game was somewhat stupid, until Kelly solved the riddle for me. "Brian, we were told she is thirteen days old. She is actually 14 days old. Do the math. What is today?" "August 7th", I replied. "Yes, its August 7th. She is a 14 day old baby girl. She has long dark hair and big brown eyes. She was born on July 24th, the same day I talked to the old man by the lake."

"My thoughts are nothing like your thoughts," says the Lord. "And my ways are far beyond anything you could imagine." Isaiah 55:8

CHAPTER 14

NOT SO SHORT TERM

Madeline Anne. What a beautiful name! The following morning, bearing gifts of formula, diapers, and wipes in hand, I came home to meet this beautiful baby girl for the first time. It was quickly evident that there was a new princess in the house, as getting the chance to hold this little bundle of joy was not the easiest task. In short order, it seemed a system of taking turns would be necessary so that all the members of our family had their chance to hold baby Maddy, as she quickly came to be called.

From the start, Maddy had quite an impact on our home. When she would cry, there would be a stampede of feet through the house, all racing to see what she needed and how they could meet that need. There were squabbles between siblings regarding who should hold her and when, whose turn it was to feed her a bottle, and who's turn it was to rock her to sleep at night. About the only thing that was never a subject of debate was whose turn it was to change her diaper!

The first weekend with Maddy in our home went by in a blur. From the time that she first came home with Kelly, we were both very upfront and honest with all our kids regarding the fact that we had been told that this would be a very short term placement in our home. Having lived the life of a foster and adoptive family, all understood, even the little ones, that Maddy would just be a short time visitor in our home. All understood as well that our job as a family over this short period of time was care for Maddy's every need and to give her all the love, affection, and attention that we possibly could. These jobs, on all accounts by everyone in our family, were accomplished with ease.

By the middle of the following week, Maddy had not left, and we were advised by Maddy's case worker that she may be staying a little while longer in our home. To be quite honest, Kelly and I were somewhat surprised by this, as it was very plainly stated when we accepted placement that this would be very short term, a couple days. But, with that being said, even though we were surprised, we were very happy to be able to enjoy her company in our home for a little while longer. Obviously, all of our kids were happy to hear this news as well.

The first week turned into the first couple weeks. Maddy was still with us. During this time, Maddy started twice per week visits with her birthmother at the agency, as the stated goal of Maddy's case plan was to be reunited with her birthmother. These first couple weeks turned into the first couple months of Maddy's life. Nothing changed. Maddy still lived in our home and visited with her birthmother twice each week. As visits continued over this time, Kelly and I both would take turns bringing Maddy to her visits with her birthmother. During this time, we started to get to know Maddy's birthmother as well. At first, to be honest, when we would meet for visits at the agency, our discussions were short, just saying "Hello" and letting Maddy's birthmother know how things had been going and how Maddy had been doing. Over time, these short "Hellos" turned into short conversations. Maddy's birthmother started to inquire about and take interest in our family and our other children, as they were acting as Maddy's foster-siblings. It became very evident to Maddy's birthmother that Maddy was very well taken care of and loved on by us all. The comfort that she took in knowing this, over time, started to build a bond between us all.

A couple months of Maddy's placement in our home turned into the first four months of her life. I distinctly remember that as time progressed, Kelly and I talked frequently amongst ourselves about our now not so short term placement. We both questioned "what is taking so long" with this relative coming to get Maddy. We wondered this more and more frequently as Christmas 2014 approached. We both were concerned, because a couple things were becoming very evident. One, was that Maddy loved her birth mother. Each and every time she would visit with her mom, she was now old enough that she would get this big smile across her face and start to babble and coo. She was excited for these visits. Secondly, it was very evident that with the amount of time spent in our home, Maddy was also becoming very attached to Kelly and me and our children. With these thoughts in mind, Kelly and I also knew through our training and education as foster parents, the agency trainers had made very clear that the importance of bonding and attachment in children cannot be overstated. In fact, we had been taught, research has shown that children experience and build the strongest, most important bonds and attachments they will ever have during their first twelve months of life. Additionally, it has been shown that if these bonds and attachments are broken in these children's lives, they are at much higher risk of developing Reactive Attachment Disorder (RAD), which, later in life, can lead to things such as anger and control issues and the inability to develop and/or maintain significant interpersonal relationships.

In light of these thoughts, during a visit in our home with Maddy's case worker around this time, we just bluntly asked the question, "Is this relative coming or not?" In reply to this question, we were advised of a couple things by Maddy's case worker: 1) the goal of Maddy's case plan was for her to be reunited with her birthmother, 2) Maddy's relative had not been returning phone calls or emails from the agency, 3) the agency, therefore, had some concerns regarding Maddy's relative, and 4) until further notice, Maddy would be staying in our home.

Christmas of 2014 was a fun time with Maddy in the house, and as we approached the New Year, Kelly and I reminisced over the past year. In doing this, we felt a great sense of accomplishment. Our family had finalized the adoptions of Kate, Trey, and Joel, all of whom seemed like they had been a part of our family forever. Additionally, we now had taken placement of a little girl who was rolling back and forth all across our living room. To say Maddy's arrival in our home was unexpected would be an understatement, but we felt very blessed to be a part of this child's life, even if it was not permanent.

As 2015 started, we continued to enjoy our Maddy time. Weekly visits continued and Kelly and I both continued to build a relationship and rapport with Maddy's birthmother, who still visited with Maddy twice each week. Four months soon turned into six months. Six months soon turned into nine. At about nine months of age, during another visit in our home with Maddy's caseworker, it was mentioned during a visit by the caseworker that Maddy's relative had again made contact with the agency and was now supposedly working on completing a home study. This, of course, caught both Kelly and I by surprise, however, as this information was relayed to us, we were also assured by the caseworker that there were no plans to move Maddy out of our home and that the goal of Maddy's case plan was still reunification with her birth mother.

Spring of 2015 turned into Summer of 2015. With the exception of Maddy continuing to get older, nothing had changed. However, in June of 2015, just a month before Maddy's first birthday, during a semi-annual case review, the agency advised us all, Maddy's birthmother included, that Maddy's relative from out of state had finally completed her home study. This news was met with concern on Kelly and my part and with outright objection on Maddy's birthmother's part. Maddy's birthmother made it very clear to all in attendance at that meeting that she never wanted her daughter to be sent out of state to live with her relative. Leaving the case review meeting at the agency that day, Kelly and I walked out with Maddy and her birthmother. I will never forget what Maddy's birthmother said that day as we left. "If I can't get her back, will you both raise my daughter? She loves you. It is obvious, and even if it means adopting her, you guys are the only ones I would want to raise her if I can't."

CHAPTER 15

BIG RED FLAG

In the following weeks leading up to Maddy's first birthday, Kelly and I had many conversations about the question that Maddy's birthmother had asked us and about the statement that she had made that day leaving the agency. We knew that the goal of the case plan had remained to reunify Maddy with her birthmother, which is something that we absolutely understood. Maddy loved her birthmother, and if it was possible, we knew that reunification was what should happen. But Kelly and I also understood Maddy's mother's concerns and her request that had been made that day. It had been almost a year that Maddy had lived in our home, and during that time, not only had Maddy bonded and attached to our family, but Kelly and I had built a strong, trusting relationship with Maddy's birthmother as well. We cared about Maddy's birthmother, she cared about Kelly and me and our family, and, above all, all of us loved and cared for Maddy. It was three adults, all of whom wanted what was best for one child, no matter what that ended up meaning.

Maddy's first birthday came and went. Maddy, of course, continued to grow and develop. No longer that cute little baby, she was now a cute little toddler who was busy walking all around, exploring her environment. August of 2015 started back-to-school preparations yet again. Milestones within our family were about to be achieved as Trey and Joel were entering kindergarten and Jay was entering high school as a freshman. Maddy continued to live in our home and visit with her birthmother twice each week.

In September of 2015, with the kids back in school and fall sports in session on an almost nightly basis, things started to change for our family and for Maddy. At a case review meeting that month, the subject of Maddy's relative resurfaced. Kelly and I were advised that the agency was preparing to initiate visits between Maddy and her relative who lived out of state. Kelly and I questioned what exactly that meant. The response of the agency was that mandated visits were going to be starting soon between Maddy and her relative. The agency also advised us that the goal of these visits was to make the introduction in order to start bonding between Maddy and this relative so that permanency could be achieved by placing Maddy with her relative out of state. This answer only brought about many more questions on our part. Isn't the goal still reunification of Maddy and her birthmother? What about Maddy's birthmother's objections to Maddy being sent out of state to live with this relative? What about the concerns Maddy's caseworker had previously expressed that the agency had about this relative? This relative has known about Maddy since the first day that she came to our home, so why haven't they been interested until now? Why hasn't this relative even so much as visited Maddy or called to talk to us and check on her or ask how she is doing? What about the bonds that have already been established with our family? Kelly and I reminded the agency representatives that the training they had given us as foster parents had taught us that the most important bonds and attachments that a child will make occur in the first 12 months of life. Maddy was now over 14 months old, and with that being the case, what about the bonds and attachments she had formed? "This relative has known about Maddy since day one, but has been totally absent since that time. Where has this relative been?" I asked. As these questions poured out, the answer we received took us back to answers we had received about Joel's relative and the Agency's decisions. It was also the answer that we would receive many more times in the coming months from the agency. "You are just foster parents. We don't have to answer your questions," we were told. After being notified of our place in the pecking order, we were advised by agency representatives to provide a couple dates over the first week of October that we were available to bring Maddy for visits with her relative.

Kelly and I left the meeting that day not knowing what to think. Hearing the news we had been told immediately felt like being hit by a ton of bricks. As we drove home that day, we discussed these circumstances at length, and we agreed that there were a couple items of grave concern. First, we felt strongly that the agency's new plans for Maddy were absolutely not in her best interests. Maddy had a bond with her birthmother. Maddy had a bond with our family as well. Maddy had no bond with this relative because there had been no effort for over a year on the part of her relative. Maddy's birthmother was estranged from the relative now seeking placement and feared if Maddy was sent there, she would never see her daughter again. This Agency plan was wrong! Second, we felt that the questions we had brought to the attention of agency representatives were absolutely appropriate questions that should be asked and needed to be answered if those involved were truly looking out for Maddy's best interests. The fact that these questions were brushed aside by agency representatives was a fact that was very troubling and spoke volumes to Kelly and me. How could someone care for a child day in and day out for over a year, but be told by Agency officials, "We don't have to answer your questions." The logic behind that response exhibited either sheer foolishness or complete disregard for a child. It was on that drive home that Kelly and I made the decision that, no matter what, we would be advocates for Maddy and her best interests. Due to Maddy's age, to the "decision makers" involved, she didn't have a voice, so Kelly and I would stand up and be her voice.

In the days that followed, we again met with Jerry Johnson, the attorney who had helped us and represented us with regard to the issues we experienced in Joel's case. Jerry took the time to listen to us and to all the facts and circumstances surrounding our case, letting us know that he would be more than happy to represent us as we advocated for the best interests of Maddy.

Kelly and I continued to do everything that was asked of us by Allen County Children Services. Even though we vehemently disagreed with the direction they were taking in Maddy's permanency planning, we also knew that, as foster parents, we had to follow the rules. As you can guess, neither of us have ever been the rule breaking type. So, as the agency had requested, we provided multiple dates in the first couple weeks of October 2015 that we were available to bring Maddy to visit her relative. Days passed, and we never received a reply. Finally, since we had heard no response, we questioned the agency when this first visit was going to happen. Their response was to tell us that we needed to provide new dates in late October for this visitation. Exasperated, we informed the agency to just schedule the visit, and we would make sure that Maddy was there, regardless of when it was scheduled. But, again, weeks went by and we received no response.

In late October 2015, at a home visit by Maddy's case worker, we were again asked to provide dates for this first visit with Maddy's relative, this time for early November. We recounted that starting in September (now over a month ago) we had on multiple occasions provided multiple dates for this visit to happen, but yet, nothing had been scheduled. We questioned, again, what is going on? Why is this taking so long? If this relative is so interested in Maddy, why have they not yet visited? Again, we were advised that as foster parents, we were not entitled to answers. Bluntly, we were told, to provide the dates and that the agency would handle scheduling a visit.

As this all continued to play out, Maddy's birthmother continued to be adamant that she did not want her daughter to visit with this relative, let alone, to be sent out of state. As the dates for these visits continued to be pushed back, Maddy's birthmother again reiterated to Kelly and me that no matter what, she wanted us to be a part of Maddy's life going forward and that if she could not get custody back, she only wanted Kelly and me to raise Maddy.

During this time as well, Kelly and I became very vocal advocates for Maddy to her guardian ad litem (GAL), Farley Banks. In these cases, the GAL serves as the court appointed attorney for the minor child. Kelly and I invited Farley to come to our home, which he did. He observed Maddy in our home environment and in her interactions with Kelly and me and our children. Farley intimated to us both that it was obvious that Maddy, the child he represented, was very well taken care of and very strongly bonded and attached within our family. Farley also understood that Maddy's birthmother was very much against any permanency planning for Maddy that involved her being sent out of state to a relative she had never, as of yet, met. He assured Kelly and me that if Maddy was not returned to her birthmother, then, as Maddy's GAL, he strongly felt it was in her best interests to remain in our home.

On October 30, 2015, Kelly and I were finally advised via email from Maddy's caseworker that Maddy would indeed now have a visit with her relative. This first visit would occur on November 4th, 2015, in a supervised setting at the agency for 1 hour. This visit would be followed by a second visit on November 9th, 2015, again supervised at the agency for 1 hour. Maddy would meet this person for the first time as she approached 16 months old.

Wednesday, November 4th, 2015, Kelly and I took Maddy to her visit at the agency. As we arrived early for the meeting, I was unsure of what to expect. Despite Kelly's and my objections to this plan for Maddy, we were determined to make the best of this situation and visit, as it would be the first time for all of us to meet her relative. Maddy's relative arrived, and introductions were made by Maddy's caseworker. After these introductions, I asked Maddy's relative if there were any questions they would like me to answer regarding Maddy. Two questions were asked that evening, and these were the only two questions that would ever be asked of either Kelly or me. "Is she allergic to anything you know of?" was the first question. I replied, "No". The second question surprised me, "Do you have any other foster kids in the house?" Again, I replied, "No". That was it. As Maddy was taken out of my arms, she started to cry. As she was taken back for this one hour visit, I knew, to me, this visit would seem to last forever.

The following week, on Monday, November 9th, 2015, this whole scenario replayed itself. The only difference was that this time, there were no questions from Maddy's relative for me to answer. And, I can tell you, this absolutely stuck out to me as a warning sign. Maddy had continually been in our care since the time she was 14 days old. She was now almost 16 months old. As I sat there that night, waiting for the visit to end, I thought to myself, questioning, "What if the roles were reversed?" If they were reversed, I would have had a ton of questions that needed to be asked and, hopefully, answered. What is Maddy's normal daily routine? Does she take a nap? What time does she go to bed? What is her favorite food? What is her favorite toy? What are her likes and dislikes? What do you do to comfort her when she is upset? Does she have a favorite blanket? I could go on and on and on. But, none of these questions had been asked. The only question I had been asked that pertained to Maddy was if she was allergic to anything. To me, this served as a BIG RED FLAG.

CHAPTER 16

ACCELERATING TIMELINE

As these visits were scheduled and took place, Maddy's birthmother, with her attorney's counsel, discussed the happenings of this case and her wishes for her daughter with our attorney. Additionally, our attorney discussed these issues with Maddy's GAL, who agreed that he was also concerned with the direction of the case and the decisions being made. In mid-November 2015, a motion was filed by our attorney with the Allen County Juvenile Court requesting that Kelly and I be granted party status in Maddy's case. Maddy's birthmother's attorney filed a motion on her behalf acknowledging her consent to Kelly and me gaining party status in the case and requesting this same court to grant us Legal Custody of her daughter. Maddy's GAL filed documents demonstrating his agreement to the above items, and requesting visitation with Maddy's out of state relative to be put on hold while the Allen County Juvenile Court considered the above motions. Kelly and I prayed that all involved would impartially consider the best interests of this little girl.

Upon being notified of the filing of motions in Maddy's case, the agency responded by pushing an accelerated timeline for visits between Maddy and her relative. After only two 1 hour supervised visits, Kelly and I were quickly notified that on November 15th and November 29th the agency had scheduled all day unsupervised visits. Maddy had literally seen this relative for a total of two hours in her entire life, and now was being mandated by the agency to be sent with them in an all day, unsupervised setting. Both of these visits were scheduled on Sundays when the agency was closed, so Kelly and I were directed that we were to bring Maddy to the agency parking lot, where we would hand Maddy over while a caseworker watched.

On Sunday, November 15th, 2015, Kelly and I, as directed, met Maddy's relative in the parking lot of Allen County Children Services to hand her off for this all day visit. Maddy's caseworker was there to supervise this hand off. I will never forget the events that occurred that day as we were forced to hand Maddy off to this person who, while a relative of hers, was a total stranger in Maddy's 16 month old mind. As one would expect, Maddy was very resistant towards interacting with, let alone going to, her relative, and every time her relative tried to take her from my arms, Maddy would latch tightly onto my arm and neck, turn her head, and repeatedly say, "No, no, no." Despite this fact, Maddy's caseworker indicated that the visit needed to proceed. Taking Maddy from my arms, her caseworker proceeded to quickly start buckling Maddy into the relative's vehicle. As soon as she realized what was occurring, Maddy started to scream and cry hysterically, alternating between yelling, "Mommy!" and "Daddy!" With there being nothing else we could do, Kelly and I both stood there and cried. As Maddy's relative left the parking lot and pulled out on the street, Kelly and I watched through the window of her vehicle as Maddy frantically tried to escape from the car seat. To this day, this event is a memory that has been seared into my mind. I can picture it just as clearly today as when I saw it happen right in front of my eyes. I will never forget what Maddy was put through that day and in the days to come.

On November 24th, 2015, Kelly and I had what would prove to be our last ever official in home visit with agency officials. During this visit with Maddy's caseworker, Yvonne Cusac, and the case supervisor, Brent Bunke, I again spoke about our concerns regarding the decisions being made by agency officials. Additionally, I highlighted what we had witnessed on November 15th and the emotional trauma and toll that we had seen exerted on Maddy. In response, I was advised by Brent Bunke, that due to our decision to obtain legal counsel, he couldn't discuss these things with us. So, yet again, we received no response from the agency regarding our questions, concerns, and the red flags we were seeing as we continued to be advocates for Maddy. Before leaving that day, however, these agency representatives informed us that Maddy was scheduled to start weekend visits out of state at her relative's home. We were told these visits would commence on the weekend of December 4th through December 6th, 2015. It was evident, due to our advocacy for what we felt were Maddy's best interests, the agency

104

was responding, not by having honest, open discussions, but only by accelerating the timeline for visitation.

November 29th came and Maddy had her next all day visit. As we arrived at the agency parking lot again that morning for the exchange, we noted that Maddy's relative was not there. Shortly after our arrival, Maddy's caseworker exited from the building and came walking towards Kelly and me. She asked us to take Maddy out of her car seat. "From this point on, Allen County Children Services representatives will be doing handoffs with Maddy," we were told. As we sat in our car in the parking lot that day, we again witnessed Maddy crying hysterically as she was loaded into an agency vehicle and taken away for this visit.

The following week, Maddy's GAL filed an ex parte motion (emergency request) with Allen County Juvenile Court requesting that these visits be stopped, as he indicated to Kelly and me that he did not believe these visits were in the best interests of his client. Surprisingly at the time (but, in retrospect – not surprising at all), the court did not move on this motion. As the agency had told us, out of state over-night visits started the weekend of December 4th through the 6th. Maddy returned from that first weekend away and we could tell something was not right. Shortly after arriving back to our home that Sunday evening, she started vomiting. She did not sleep well. Her mood and sleeping patterns changed. Over the next couple of days, we noticed and documented that she had gone from a child that slept all night, every night, to a child who woke up crying multiple times through the night. This lasted until Thursday that week, when she finally again slept through the night.

The following two weekends, December 11th though the 13th and December 18th through the 20th, Maddy again was picked up at our home and escorted out of state for weekend visits with her relative. Each time she was picked up at our home, we witnessed a crying, devastated, hysterical child being picked up by a random agency caseworker who was a stranger to her, only to be dropped off in an unknown location to yet another person who was a stranger to her. Each time she would come back to our home, we saw the repeated patterns of mood changes, Maddy not wanting to eat, not feeling well, and having vastly disturbed sleep patterns, all of which would last for 3 or 4 days. Kelly and I documented this and we notified the agency caseworker of this, yet the agency refused discussions pertaining to what we were witnessing. Disturbed and searching for answers, Kelly and I consulted with a pediatric psychologist. When told of what was going on in Maddy's life and the effects we were witnessing, this psychologist equated the trauma she was being put through to what, in Maddy's mind, would be equivalent to repeated kidnappings. Throughout this entire time, Maddy continued to visit with her birthmother twice weekly at the agency. Maddy's birthmother continued to tell the agency that she wanted the visits to stop and she wanted Kelly and me to raise Maddy. And throughout this entire time, the motion Maddy's GAL had filed requesting to stop out of state visits was not acted on by the Allen County Juvenile Court.

Maddy returned home on Sunday, December 20th, 2015, with no further visits being scheduled. It was mentioned by Maddy's caseworker that the agency was attempting to schedule an out of state visit over New Year's weekend, but for reasons we were never told, this visit never materialized. Kelly and I and our family enjoyed and treasured every minute we spent with Maddy over Christmas and New Years. I can attest to the simple truth that not knowing how much longer you have with someone will make you treasure every minute you have with them. That is a lesson I have tried to remember and apply to all those I love each and every day since, because in reality, we just never know. Don't take those minutes and times together for granted!

As we moved towards the end of 2015, we were advised that Allen County Juvenile Court had finally assigned a court date of January 8th, 2016, for hearing the numerous motions that had been filed in Maddy's case. As this date approached, we eagerly awaited the chance to be advocates for this child in a court room. Kelly and I met again with Maddy's GAL, who advised us that he did not believe any of this Agency plan currently taking place was in Maddy's best interests, further stating that if Maddy was not to be reunited with her birthmother, then he believed that her best interests were served by permanent placement in our home. He reiterated that he had seen how bonded and attached Maddy, his client, was to our family.

On January 4th, 2016, just days before our court hearing, Allen County Children Services filed a motion in the Allen County Juvenile Court requesting Legal Custody of Maddy be granted to her relative. Keep in mind, this motion was made despite all the questions and concerns we had raised, despite the protests of Maddy's birthmother and Maddy's GAL, and despite the fact that Maddy had only ever interacted with this person on two occasions for one hour each, on two more occasions for 6 hours each time, and for 6 additional days, all spread out over the preceding two months. Comparatively, Maddy, now almost 18 months old, had lived in our home for all but the first two weeks of her life.

January 8th, 2016 arrived. In court that day, testimony was given by Maddy's birthmother and her GAL in support of Kelly and me being given party status in Maddy's case. They both attested to the fact that they felt this was in Maddy's best interests. Maddy's birthmother testified that Maddy looked at Kelly and me as her "mom and dad" and that she only wanted Maddy to be raised in our home even if that meant we were given Legal Custody. Of course, the agency argued against this, and requested the court to give Legal Custody to Maddy's relative. At the close of the hearing that day, it was ordered by the court that final closing arguments would be written and due to the court on January 29th, 2016.

The week following this hearing, I personally met again with Farley Banks, Maddy's GAL, to continue to discuss our concerns as they related to Maddy. Sitting across the desk from him that day in his office, he proceeded to tell me that he had, "really got my butt chewed because of the stance I have taken to support Maddy being with you guys." I responded by thanking him for doing what he felt was in the best interests of the child he represented and for doing what was right.

After a 3 week hiatus, out of state visits were again scheduled by the agency. Maddy was scheduled to visit January 15th through the 17th, January 22nd through the 24th, and January 29th through the 31st. After both of the first two of these weekend long visits, Kelly and I again witnessed and documented Maddy's changes in mood, eating habits, and sleep disturbances. As before, these changes would last 3 or 4 days, go away, then restart again when she was returned home after the next subsequent visit. For some unknown reason Maddy's out of state visit, scheduled for the last weekend in January 2016, was cancelled.

Final closing arguments from the January 8th court date had been turned into the court on January 29th, so as we entered February 2016, Kelly and I waited with anticipation for the ruling of the Allen County Juvenile Court. As Maddy continued to visit twice weekly with her birthmother, it was our hope that soon all this turmoil would come to an end. However, on Wednesday, February 10th, 2016, Kelly and I received a phone call that I will never forget. In fact, I have saved the voicemail from this call on my phone ever since as a reminder to never lose the resolve to do what is right, no matter who that may offend or anger. That night, via phone, Farley Banks, Maddy's GAL, reversed course. He advised Kelly and I that he would be changing his recommendation to the court by submitting a new GAL's report recommending that Maddy be sent to live with her out of state relative and that her relative be named Legal Custodian by the court. Upon hearing this news, it was very evident the direction that things were heading. We consulted with our attorney and Maddy's birthmother consulted with hers. All came to the conclusion that the writing was on the wall, so to speak, and at this point, Maddy's birthmother again asked if we would be willing to adopt her daughter. Of course, Kelly and I again said, "Yes".

Maddy had been sent out of state for a visit the weekend of February 5th through the 7th. The following two visits scheduled for February 12th through the 14th and February 19th through the 21st were again cancelled. On February 24th, Kelly and I received an email that there would be a weekend visit scheduled for February 26th though February 28th. We were also told that the evening of February 28th, when Maddy was returned to our home, Maddy's caseworker would need to meet with us. During this meeting we were told by Maddy's caseworker that the agency was moving Maddy out of our home to her out of state relative within the next two weeks. I personally asked her how the agency could do this while we were still waiting on the court to rule on all the motions that were filed. Maddy's caseworker responded, "We are the agency. We can and will do what we want."

Two days later, on March 1, 2016, the Allen County Juvenile Court issued its ruling denying Kelly's and my motion for party status in Maddy's case. In this denial, the court stated that Kelly and I becoming party to Maddy's case was NOT in her best interests. Additionally, in this ruling the court scheduled a Legal Custody hearing for

Maddy to be held on May 26th and 27th, 2016, at which time it would take into consideration whether to grant the agency's motion requesting Legal Custody to be given to Maddy's relative or Maddy's birthmother's motion requesting Legal Custody to be awarded to Kelly and me. Of note, this ruling was time stamped by the court as being issued at 3:53 p.m. Just seven minutes after this time stamp, Kelly and I received an email from the agency advising us that Maddy would be permanently removed from our home and sent out of state on March 16th, 2016, which, coincidentally or not, was also Kelly's birthday.

With these agency plans now on full display, Maddy's birthmother, with her own legal counsel, made an adoptive plan for her daughter. She again asked Kelly and me, making sure that we would adopt, if given the opportunity. We, of course, said, "Yes." Kelly and I discussed these plans and the process of things to follow with our attorney. Our attorney met with Maddy's birthmother's attorney. These attorneys attempted to discuss with the agency what was now going to be a pending adoption. They requested that the pending removal of Maddy from our home be placed on hold. The agency refused to cooperate with these requests. As March 16th, 2016, approached, Kelly and I both felt like we were drowning. It is hard to describe all the emotions that swirled, but I can tell you that I questioned God a lot during this time. What I was about to learn is that we don't always get the answers to prayer that we want, but that doesn't mean that God is not there with us every step along the way.

I will call upon your name,

And keep my eyes above the waves,

When oceans rise,

My soul will rest in your embrace.

"Oceans" by Hillsong United

CHAPTER 17

GONE

Wednesday, March 16, 2016, Kelly and I were instructed to bring Maddy to the agency for the second of her weekly visits with her birth mother. We were told that we needed to drop her off at the agency that morning, then leave town. Agency representatives did not want us around, as it had been decided by those in charge, both Brent Bunke and agency director Cynthia Scanland, that Maddy would be taken out of state at the conclusion of this visit to live with her relative. Despite Maddy's birthmother's protests, despite all the concerns and red flags that Kelly and I had brought to the attention of the agency, despite the pending adoption, these persons had decided that Maddy was leaving our home, and in their minds, this was a permanent move.

I can vividly remember that day. Driving to the agency, Kelly and I both sat quietly. We were both sick to our stomach over what was about to happen. Maddy, now just shy of 20 months old, was the only sound in the car as she filled the void left by our lack of conversation with her constant chatter. It seemed like every day, she learned a new word or short phrase, and that day, it seemed like she wanted to remind us of all the words she knew, which made this trip all the more difficult. Our minds raced, our attitudes sank, and our hearts broke as we neared the agency. Kelly and I didn't want to display our emotions in front of Maddy, as she knew she was going to visit her birthmother and was happy for these visits. Maddy continued to babble and talk, and about a block away from the agency, not knowing when we might see her again, Kelly and I both, while fighting back tears, told Maddy we loved her. I will never forget her reply, as it was the first time either of us had heard her string these words together, "I luhh Mommy," she said, shortly thereafter followed by, "I luhh Daddy." Instantly, tears started to flow. Shortly thereafter, we dropped Maddy off at the agency. As we met out in the lobby, Maddy excitedly ran to the waiting arms of her birthmother, oblivious to the events that would soon take place in her life.

Little did Kelly and I know what was to come as well. Our former attorney, Jerry Johnson, had recommended that we go to a colleague of his, Susan Eisenman, for representation in this pending adoption. Susan had advised Kelly and me she felt that within a matter of weeks, Maddy would potentially be back in our home through pre-adoptive placement. In saying that, she had also cautioned us that this adoption could also turn into a case where the agency tried to drag things out in the court system, and, if that was the route they chose to take, then it could, obviously, prolong the expected timeline. On March 16th, 2016, Kelly and I never would have imagined that we would be prohibited from seeing our daughter for more than 7 months.

In the weeks following Maddy's removal from our home, many things transpired. Maddy's birthmother, through her attorney, petitioned the agency for visitation rights. As the Ohio Revised Code states, the right of a birth parent is to have visitation with their child, and Maddy had been moved out of state to a location three and a half hours away. The agency, in their infinite knowledge and wisdom, granted visitation rights for Maddy's birthmother, but knowing that Maddy's birthmother had no vehicle and/or transportation, they only granted visitation once per week, out of state, over a three and a half hour drive away. Kelly and I knew how important visitation was between Maddy and her birthmother. We knew that there was a strong bond and attachment there that needed to be maintained for Maddy's well being. We also saw the game that the agency was playing…..if birthmother doesn't show for visits, the result is her testimony to the court regarding the wishes she has for her daughter is diminished. So, with all those factors in mind, Kelly and I made the commitment to Maddy's birthmother that we would make sure that she always had transportation to and from the out of state visitation that had been concocted by the agency, a seven hour round trip in total.

As this visitation started to take place, Maddy's birthmother did make inquiry of the agency whom exactly she was allowed to bring to her visits with her daughter. The agency responded that she could bring anyone she wanted – family or friend – as long as they had had the required background check and fingerprinting done prior to the visit. In response, Maddy's birthmother notified agency officials that both Kelly and I were already background checked and fingerprinted, and since we were taking her to her out of state visits, she wanted us to participate in the visits with her. The agency responded by advising her that the "anyone" they had referred to actually meant anyone but the Andersons.

With the issues that we had run into near the completion of Joel's adoption, Kelly and I had thought we had seen it all. As I stated earlier, the issues we encountered back then had really soured us towards the inner workings of the agency. What we soon found out, however, was that we hadn't even began to scratch the surface of the worst that we would see. As we moved into the waning days of March 2016, we were about to get our eyes opened to this fact even more.

Despite Maddy having been removed from our home and moved out of state, the adoption process continued to move forward. The Ohio Revised Code clearly states that adoptions can be heard only in the Probate Court system. Additionally, it is outlined that the appropriate venues for Probate Courts to hear adoptions include courts in the county in which the child was born, the county in which the birth parent resides, or the county in which the prospective adoptive parents reside. Having been residents of Mercer County, Ohio, our entire lives, Kelly and I had applied for our adoption of Maddy in Mercer County Probate Court. We were scheduled for a pre-adoptive placement hearing in Mercer County Probate Court on March 31st, 2016.

Present at this hearing were Maddy's birthmother, Kelly and I, and our attorney. Maddy's birthmother's attorney was not able to attend the hearing that day, but provided a certified letter to the Probate Court stating that he had discussed this adoption in detail with his client and that, in consultation with his client, attested to the fact that this is what she wanted for her daughter and that she was fully aware of what our adoption of Maddy would mean.

That day, we all provided testimony to the Mercer County Probate Judge regarding each of our individual reasons for wanting this adoption to take place. Kelly and I have no idea what was said between Maddy's birthmother and the Judge because we were asked to wait outside the court room while this discussion took place. For our part, we confirmed to the Judge that Maddy had been removed from our home just two weeks prior, and we informed the Judge that we loved Maddy as much as any of our other children, stating that Maddy's removal from our home had felt like a death in the family. We also informed the Judge that we cared for Maddy's birthmother and had long ago been asked by her to raise her daughter if she couldn't achieve reunification. After all parties had individually testified in front of the Mercer County Probate Court that day, the Judge, Mary Pat Zitter, called us all into her court room together.

Judge Zitter proceeded to notify us all that she wished that more often she would see three adults so focused and concerned with the best interest of a child who had been a part of all their lives. She informed us that it was very obvious to her that we all only wanted what we felt was best for this little child and that this child was blessed to have us all in her life. She closed the hearing by confirming that as the Probate Judge in Mercer County, the adoption petition was properly in front of her court, that Maddy's birthmother did have the right per the Ohio Revised Code to consent to and cause placement of her child for adoption, that she (Judge Zitter) was vested with the authority to determine this adoption in her court, and that she had concluded from all the testimony and evidence presented that it was absolutely in Maddy's best interests that this adoption move forward. We left Mercer County Probate Court that day with a signed adoptive placement order in hand which stated in part,

"The Court, upon consideration of all the evidence and testimony of the applicant who appeared in Court, finds that such placement would be for the best interest of said child. THEREFORE, IT IS THE ORDER OF THE COURT that such proposed placement be, and the same hereby is approved, that the applicant be authorized to cause such placement to be made forthwith, and that adoption proceedings may go forth in this Court. IT IS FURTHER ORDERED that Allen County Children Services release the infant to the attorney for the adoptive parents, Susan Eisenman."

A feeling of relief washed over us all, however, this saga was far from over.

CHAPTER 18

#BRINGMADDYHOME

The following day, April 1, 2016, Allen County Children Services, through their attorney in the Allen County Prosecutors Office, filed an emergency motion in Allen County Juvenile Court requesting an order from that court to prevent Maddy from being returned to us as outlined in the adoptive placement order issued the previous day in Mercer County. Without a hearing on the matter, the Allen County Juvenile Court Judge Glenn Derryberry agreed to this request and issued an order asserting his perceived jurisdiction in this case stating, "*IT IS THEREFORE ORDERED, consistent with the prior orders of this Court, that the Allen County Children's Services Board has the right to the physical care and control of the minor child, Madeline Anne Spurlock and is entitled to determine where and with whom the child shall live. IT IS FURTHER ORDERED that the child is not to be relocated from the placement made by the Allen County Children's Services Board under the statutory authority with which it is vested pending further order of this court.*" With the support provided by this ruling issued by Judge Derryberry, Allen County Children Services would continue to refuse to return Maddy to Kelly and me.

This is just the first of many legal filings and rulings that would take place over the following months. Throughout the month of April, Allen County Children Services refused many things, the most important of which was to return Maddy to Kelly and me. Despite numerous attempts by our lawyer to meet with Allen County Children Services leaders and their attorney, these officials refused to meet to discuss the law, specifics of the Ohio Revised Code, and possible pathways to a settlement of this issue of adoption that would not involve a long, drawn out court battle. As days passed by, Kelly and I still were denied access to or visitation with Maddy.

Having an adoptive placement order in hand in Ohio means a couple of things for the pre-adoptive parents named on the order. First, it means that a Probate Court, the court system vested in Ohio with the authority to determine best interests and approve or deny adoptions, has found that it is in the child's best interests to be adopted by the parties named for adoptive placement. Secondly, per the Ohio Revised Code, an adoptive placement order gives the parties named, in this case Kelly and I, the right to care, control, and custody of the child pending finalization of the proposed adoption {ORC 5103.16(D)(3)}. This being the case, Kelly and I became increasingly frustrated. Despite a court order, we were still being denied access to Maddy. The fact was that an Ohio governmental agency was doing anything they could to thwart a valid order of an Ohio Probate Court. Feeling that we had been backed into a corner by a tax payer supported agency with an unlimited amount of tax payer funded attorneys at their disposal, Kelly and I made a decision that we never have regretted.

We decided to get very loud and vocal about our case. We decided that we would not back down and silently slink back into the shadows as we were battered about by this agency. As the persons who had been granted care, control, and custody of Maddy on March 31st in Mercer County Probate Court, we decided that we would speak openly and freely about our case, that we would be advocates for change in a broken system that was attempting to prevent our adoption of Maddy, and that we would use today's social media outlets to spread far and wide our story, Maddy's story, thereby shining a light on an agency that wanted to hide behind their perceived cloak of confidentiality. To the chagrin of the agency, #BringMaddyHome was born.

As it became very evident that Allen County Children Services, with the support of their Juvenile Court Judge, were going to go to whatever lengths they could to prevent our adoption of Maddy, our attorney advised us that this could be a lengthy affair. With that in mind, we requested both agency officials and the Allen County Juvenile Court to grant us visitation with Maddy as the legal process in this case played out. After all, Kelly and I were transporting Maddy's birthmother to her weekly out-of-state visitation with Maddy. Additionally, Maddy's birthmother had already requested that the agency allow Kelly and I to participate in visitation with her. Despite these facts, and despite the fact that Kelly and I had obtained a signed adoptive placement order which called for Maddy to be returned to us, Allen County Officials refused to allow Kelly and I to participate in the once per week visits with Maddy. As weeks passed, each and every week, we were forced to sit in a parking lot, mere spectators, as Maddy played with her birthmother in a fenced in playground just 50 yards away from where we sat.

With the passing of these weeks, #BringMaddyHome took off as our story was spread on social media. To be honest, prior to this, I had never fully realized the reach of this platform, but it seemed as if each day, we had a constant stream of people reaching out to our family, letting us know that they supported us and were praying for Maddy and our family. Some of these people, of course, were family members and friends, but many of these people were persons whom Kelly and I didn't even know. Obviously, the agency did not appreciate the attention that the #BringMaddyHome campaign was bringing. Our attorney was advised that Kelly and I had signed confidentiality agreements as foster parents, and that our social media campaign and public speaking about our case was in violation of these agreements. In response, our attorney reminded them that we were no longer the foster parents of Maddy, but rather, we were the pre-adoptive parents of Maddy and, as such, the adoptive placement order issued by the Probate Court – the one the agency was refusing to obey – gave us sole care, control, and custody of Maddy pending finalization of our adoption.

In early May of 2016, with the flurry of court filings that had taken place in the preceding month, Mercer County Probate Court had issued a ruling analyzing the Ohio Revised Code. In its analysis of relevant Revised Code statutes, the Probate Court highlighted the occurrences in Maddy's case, how these related to the pathway laid out in the Ohio Revised Code for both the Juvenile Court and Probate Court system, and the standing by which the Ohio Revised Code gave the Probate Court the ability to assume jurisdiction over Maddy's pending adoption in this case. With these facts and supporting details laid out, the Probate Court granted our request for a Contempt of Court motion against Allen County Children Services for failing to return Maddy to our home, as had been demanded by the adoptive placement order that had been issued by the Probate Court.

In my opinion, with a looming contempt of court hearing and sensing that the Probate Court was not going to tolerate the legal game of chicken the agency was playing with Maddy hanging in the balance, Allen County Children Services represented by the Allen County Prosecutors Office appealed this case to the Ohio Supreme Court on May 10th, 2016 (Ohio Supreme Court Case #2016-0723). Our attorney, in response, submitted an appeal on our behalf to the Ohio Supreme Court on May 16th, 2016 (Ohio Supreme Court Case #2016-0763).

In late May, with these appeals still pending before the Ohio Supreme Court, for the first time in a long time, Kelly and I received communication from Allen County Children Services. This communication came through US Mail and informed us that Allen County Children Services was recommending to the Ohio Department of Job and Family Services that Kelly's and my certification as a state approved foster home be revoked. Their basis for this recommendation stated, in relevant part, as follows:

Records and Confidentiality

    The Anderson's violated the confidentiality of a foster child and her family to persons not directly involved in the child's care and treatment. Disclosures of case specific, confidential information and photos of the child lead to a social media firestorm on multiple platforms including: Facebook, Twitter, Instagram, and Google Plus. The breach of confidentiality on social media lead to the creation of (hashtag) #BringMaddyHome. The breach of confidentiality continues on a frequent basis. Supporters of #BringMaddyHome publicly posted the home addresses of two supervisors and the assigned caseworker. Shortly after the postings, the caseoworker's home was vandalized and a note was left threatening the caseworker's two young children. Another employee's property was damaged. The Anderson's have held numerous fundraisers to support their legal fees to have a foster child returned to their home against the Allen County Juvenile Court, who holds jurisdiction. The Anderson's hired a private investigator to examine the foster child's (relative). The Anderson's have publicly shared on social media that ACCS sent the foster child to her (relative's) residence, a home with "drugs, sexual exploits, and security cameras because of family members stealing".

Let me start out by first saying, the claims of vandalism, threats, and property damage are to this day, unsubstantiated claims. There was a police report filed in a neighboring county regarding supposed threats with fingers being pointed at Kelly and me and #BringMaddyHome supporters. In light of this, Kelly and I offered to come in and meet with the local law enforcement agency officials to whom the report had been made. These law enforcement officials advised us that it would not be necessary. Other than that false accusation, all the above was true. What Allen County Children Services was failing to consider or recognize, however, was the standing that an order of adoptive placement gave to Kelly and me. Ohio Revised Code 5103.16 (D)(3) specifically states, "If the court approves a placement, the prospective adoptive parent(s) with whom the child is placed has care, control, and custody of the child pending further order of the court." Therefore, we were no longer the foster parents of Maddy, and, per the law, the agency did not have care, control, and custody of our child. As the agency that refused to abide by this court order and/or recognize Ohio law and the subsequent status that the order of Mercer County Probate Court had given to Kelly and me, Allen County Children Services had made up their mind that Kelly and I were now unfit to be certified foster parents in the state of Ohio. Allen County Children Services was making it clear that they were going to attempt to put a stop to this adoption, and that they were going to prevent our family from ever fostering another child.

With this notification, Kelly and I were given two options. We were advised that we could voluntarily withdraw from the process by signing and returning paperwork that was included with the notification, therefore voluntarily giving up our family's certification as a foster home. Alternatively, we were advised that we did have the right to proceed through a grievance process. As you can guess, we were not about to back down from this agency and its attempted continued harassment of our family. I researched the grievance process that was available. In short, we had the right to grieve the revocation attempt by Allen County Children Services. If we proceeded with the grievance, our response and the circumstances surrounding the action would be reviewed and researched at the local agency level. At the end of this review, findings of the reviewer would be forwarded to the Allen County Children Services Director, Cynthia Scanland, who would then make a determination whether to proceed with revocation of our license or not. If the agency Director made the decision to continue with revocation of our foster license, Kelly and I would then have the right to request a hearing on this matter at the State level.

The decision on what path to take was simple. Kelly and I contested the attempted revocation of our foster license. We proceeded through the grievance process as outlined. In our grievance response, we detailed, in a four page letter the numerous issues and concerns that we had with the agency and the decisions they had made, the deception we had witnessed, and the lies we had been told surrounding both Joel's case and Kate and Trey's case. We referenced our history with the agency as both foster parents and adoptive parents including the numerous, glowing reviews we had received as foster care providers for this agency. We reminded the agency that in the past, Kelly and I had even been invited to come in and help with the training provided to new foster parents completing their certification coursework. We highlighted the serious concerns we held in regard to the agency's decisions with Maddy and their current choice for her placement. We touched again on the concerning information we had uncovered regarding this home where she was currently placed. We reminded the agency of the questions we had asked that they had failed to answer. We asked the agency to thoroughly investigate the concerns we raised in our grievance so that, in the future, other children, families, and foster families would not be subjected to the same deception and manipulation. We welcomed the agency to move forward with this proposed revocation of our foster license, because we had so much to discuss if we had the opportunity to go to a hearing at the State level.

As you may have guessed, Kelly and I would never again hear anything more regarding this attempted revocation of our foster license. It went away, disappeared. In the following months, we would ask the agency the status of this pending revocation, however, we never received an answer, other than to inform us that it was under review. I believe this enforces a great point that I have always tried to remember. None of us should ever be afraid to stand up for what is right. To be honest, at this point, Kelly and I knew that we were "done" being foster parents. But, even with that being the case, this bogus action taken against us by an agency that was trying to bully us into walking away from foster care was not right. Although it never materialized, we relished the idea of having an open hearing at the state level to discuss not just our situation, but the state of foster care in Ohio as a whole. To that end, moving forward, Kelly and I realized that the system will not change on its own. Outside forces must take action in order to bring about change. Therefore, we have become active in policy discussions with our elected officials. Needless to say, reform does need to happen, and we are actively pursuing this agenda, which I will discuss later in this book.

As the end of May 2016 approached, Mercer County Probate Court had scheduled a contempt hearing for Friday, June 3rd. Kelly and I were happy that the Probate Judge, having already provided his legal analysis of the circumstances of the case and the relevant sections of the Ohio Revised Code, was planning to move forward in an effort to enforce the adoptive placement order that had been issued. Our family missed Maddy immensely. We had not seen her for over two months at this point. Despite our requests and Maddy's birthmother's request, the agency had refused to even allow us to visit with Maddy. However, with the Probate Court intending to proceed on the adoption case, we felt things were moving in the right direction. Kelly and I talked about how we were beginning to feel as if there was a light at the end of the tunnel. But, as we were about to find out, just because a storm subsides a little, does not mean the storm is ending.

"When you go through deep waters, I will be with you."
Isaiah 43:2

CHAPTER 19

FINDING FAITH

May 31st, 2016, is a day that I will never forget, for it was on this date that I learned just how far this agency and its leadership were willing to go to protect their own interests, rather than that of a child.

On this day, Kelly and I both traveled together taking Maddy's birthmother to her weekly scheduled visit. Since the agency would not let us participate in these visits, Kelly and I dropped Maddy's birthmother off, and we proceeded to go to the local Applebee's restaurant to get some dinner. We had both just started eating our salads when Kelly's phone rang. Expecting it to be a phone call from one of our kids at home, Kelly, surprised, told me it was Maddy's birthmother calling. As she answered the phone, the look on her face as she listened said it all…..something was wrong. After hanging up, Kelly said, "Let's go, I will explain on the way back there." I would find out from Kelly on our drive back to the visitation center, Maddy's birthmother's visit had started out well but after a short time, she started to notice some concerning issues. These things caused her to investigate further, and in the end, she had noted that Maddy had head lice knits, numerous bruises and abrasions, a terrible, bleeding diaper rash, and what looked like a round burn in the palm of her hand. She had indicated to Kelly that she was going to ask that law enforcement be called to investigate, because she was very concerned with what she was seeing.

As we pulled back into the parking lot, Kelly and I quickly noticed that there were already law enforcement vehicles there. We waited outside for what seemed like forever, worrying about our little girl, but knowing nothing of what was going on inside. After a while, we saw Maddy's relative pull back into the visitation center parking lot. As she marched into the building, we could see that she was talking very animatedly into her phone. A short while later, this relative exited the building carrying Maddy out to the waiting car. They were followed by a couple sheriff deputies, who watched as Maddy was placed in her car seat, then followed Maddy's relative as she pulled out of the parking lot and headed down the street. Shortly thereafter, Maddy's birthmother exited the building and got into our car. Immediately, she broke down crying. She told us that she couldn't believe what she had seen and that she was worried for Maddy. She indicated that when law enforcement had arrived, she showed them the items of concern, asking that Maddy get checked out by a physician to make sure everything was alright. These officers agreed that Maddy should be checked out. They took photos and called Maddy's relative to come back and pick her up, with directions to take her straight to the local hospital emergency room for a medical evaluation by a physician. Maddy's birthmother had received their assurance that they would follow Maddy to the hospital and request that she be medically evaluated.

The 3 ½ hour drive home that evening was very quiet. We all were concerned for Maddy. None of us knew for sure what was going on. We had to rely on faith that Maddy's Heavenly Father was watching over her.

Later that night, after we had all arrived back to our respective homes, Kelly and I received another phone call from Maddy's birthmother. We had been expecting this call, as she had told us that as soon as she heard anything about Maddy's medical evaluation, she would call and let us know. Yet again, the news we heard was very unexpected and quite troubling, as it turned out that Maddy had not been medically evaluated. Law enforcement had explained that since Allen County Children Services had temporary custody of Maddy, no medical evaluation could take place without their consent. Upon arriving at the local ER that evening, Maddy had been checked in and registered as a patient, however, Allen County Children Services had called and spoken with the sheriffs department deputies and hospital staff and refused to give consent for Maddy to be medically evaluated. Their directions to the officials involved were to not proceed with the physician evaluation, to send Maddy home with her relative, and that the agency would then send someone out the following day to check on Maddy. Yes, you read that right.....from out of state, over the phone, this agency denied Maddy a medical evaluation that both her birthmother and the law enforcement officials that had been called that night agreed that she needed! Hearing this news, Kelly and I were speechless. Based on the legitimate concerns that were present, we could not believe that this agency would go so far as to deny Maddy the right to a medical evaluation, but that is exactly what had happened.

The morning that followed, we were filled with fear and worry. Questions, like the waves of a tsunami, washed over us. Is Maddy OK? Why was she denied a medical evaluation? How can an agency deny this evaluation over the phone from out of state? What are they trying to hide? As these questions rolled in, we held onto the hope that Maddy would soon be back in our arms. We were just a day away from a contempt hearing scheduled for June 2, 2016, in Mercer County Probate Court, that we hoped would force the agency to comply with the court order that demanded Maddy be returned to us. But sometimes in our lives, storms continue to build, and that would be the case for Kelly and me, as on June 1st, the day after this visit where Maddy was denied medical evaluation and the day before the contempt hearing, the Ohio Supreme Court would speak for the first time with regard to the appeals that had been filed in our adoption of Maddy. This day, the Ohio Supreme Court placed a stay on Mercer County Probate Court stating, *"Respondents (Mercer County Probate Court) are hereby prohibited from exercising jurisdiction in the case captioned In the Matter of the Placement and Adoption of M.A.S.A, Mercer County Common Pleas Court, Probate Division, Case No. 2016-5005, consistent with the opinion to follow."* In plain English, the Ohio Supreme Court had prohibited Mercer County Probate Court from proceeding with hearings in Maddy's adoption case, pending the Ohio Supreme Court's opinion which would come later. Our adoption of Maddy was on hold.

Following this Ohio Supreme Court directive, Mercer County filed a motion for reconsideration to the Ohio Supreme Court, asking them to reconsider the order that had been issued. We were advised that it could be quite some time before a response was received. As we moved through the month of June, Kelly and I continued to just try to take things one day at a time. We continued taking Maddy's birthmother each and every week to her scheduled out-of-state visits. We continued to be prohibited by the agency from participating in these visits. Soon, it had been over 3 months since we had last seen Maddy. As hard as this was on Kelly and me, I would be remiss if I neglected to relate the effect this had on our children as well. Maddy had been in their lives since she was 14 days old for a period of almost 20 months. Breah, Jay, Aiden, Alex, Kate, Trey, and Joel all looked at Maddy as their sister. Their love for her as a foster-sister was no different than if she had been born to us. And while, obviously depending on the individual age of each child, their understanding of this case and proceedings in our adoption of Maddy differed somewhat, they all knew that Maddy's birthmother wanted our family to adopt her daughter, and they all understood that the agency was trying to prevent this adoption. This fact, was the cause of some very sleepless nights, especially for Kate, Trey, and Joel, who were new enough to being adopted that they still remembered their time as foster children in our home. For our part, Kelly and I took their concerns very seriously. We frequently tried to explain, in terms that they would understand, that their adoptions were all finalized meaning they never had to leave. Breah, Jay, Aiden, and Alex also did their part, assuring Kate, Trey, and Joel that they were their "sister and brothers" and there was nothing that would ever change that fact.

The beginning of July approached and, while Mercer County Probate Court had received instruction not to proceed with hearings in our case, Allen County Juvenile Court had not received any directions pertaining to their hearings, so the Juvenile Court had proceeded with scheduling a Legal Custody hearing in Maddy's case for July 12th and 13th, 2016. At issue for this hearing was the competing requests of Allen County Children Services, who had requested the Juvenile Court to give Legal Custody of Maddy to her relative, and Maddy's birthmother, who had requested the Juvenile Court to give Legal Custody of her daughter to Kelly and me.

This hearing did indeed last the two full days for which it was scheduled. Kelly and I, who had been denied our request for party status in Allen County Juvenile Court, were barred from sitting in on the hearing, with the exception of each of our individual times that we were called to the stand as witnesses. My time on the stand lasted less than one hour. I got off easy. Kelly, on the other hand, testified for over two hours. During Kelly's testimony, Maddy's birthmother's attorney questioned her regarding her love and care for Maddy, her relationship that had been built with Maddy's birthmother, and her concern regarding the agency's decisions in Maddy's case. The Allen County Prosecutor who was representing the agency at this hearing, Jurgen Waldick, took a different direction in questioning Kelly however. For over an hour, he badgered her about her vocal stance and public statements regarding Maddy's case. In my opinion, he tried to scare and intimidate my wife during her time on the stand, referencing, in his opinion, the contract as a foster parent that she had violated and the subsequent repercussions she could experience due to these alleged breaches of confidentiality. He informed Kelly that we were just foster parents and we were not the ones who got to ask questions of the agency, which we had already heard multiple times before. Honestly, in retrospect, it seems to me that Mr. Waldick was more concerned with lecturing Kelly and trying to intimidate her than he was in actually asking pertinent questions in an attempt to find out what may be in the best interests of Maddy with regard to her placement. Little did he realize that day as Kelly took the stand, that his bullying tactics, his threats, and his attempted intimidation of my wife would never work. You see, the day the agency removed Maddy from our home, despite our pending adoption hearing, Allen County Children Services had already done the worst thing imaginable to Kelly and me and our family. Nothing else the Allen County Prosecutor could threaten to do to my wife would hold a candle to what had already been done.

At the close of this two day hearing, the Juvenile Court Judge, Glenn Derryberry, determined that, after all the testimony that had taken place, written closing arguments would be submitted to the court and that these written closing arguments would be due August 26th, 2016. So, again, it became a waiting game, as we would be forced to wait until the end of August for the close of the hearing, then we would still have to wait longer for Judge Derryberry's decision regarding Legal Custody of Maddy.

Kelly and I continued to wait. By the middle of August, we had not seen Maddy in 5 months. We continued to take Maddy's birthmother to her weekly out-of-state visits. We continued to be refused visitation with Maddy. As you can imagine, this process really started to wear on us. It seemed like every week mirrored the 1993 movie "Ground Hog Day", where Phil the weatherman is destined to re-live the same day over and over again. The difference was, Kelly and I re-lived the same process on a weekly basis. We waited for courts to make rulings, we did not see Maddy, we traveled out-of-state, we worried and worried, not knowing when this process would ever end as well as not knowing when or if we would ever see our daughter again.

As late August approached, written closing arguments were being made difficult because the Juvenile Court had not yet issued the requested transcript of the Legal Custody hearing, due, as we were told, to a backup caused by vacations being taken. With that as the backdrop, the due date for these written closing arguments in the Legal Custody case, and thus the end of the Legal Custody case, was pushed back to the end of September 2016. It was another delay that would continue to keep our family from being reunited with Maddy.

As Kelly and I ate dinner one night in early September while Maddy's birthmother had a visit, on what had become sarcastically known to our children as "mom and dad's out-of-state date nights", we had a conversation that I will never forget. During this conversation, we discussed in detail all that had happened since the day we had first met little Madeline Anne. We discussed the highs and lows we had both felt throughout our time with Maddy and in the time since she had been taken from our home. We discussed all we had been through and how each day it seemed more and more difficult to keep moving forward. We discussed the impact this case had had on our family, our finances, our relationship, and our faith. We both freely admitted that, at times, we had questioned God in the preceding months. Why would He would bring this little child into our life? Why would her birthmother choose to ask us to adopt her? Why was she ripped away from all she had ever known? Was she doing OK? If we could adopt her, would she remember us? Would the events of her life that she had no control over traumatize her? We had so many questions, but there were so few answers. But, sitting there that night, we decided to stop asking questions. Instead, we both decided to lay out what we did know, and we agreed that we would stand united on a simple set of facts:

- **God is in control.**
- **We have done what He has asked us to do.**
- **We have done everything within our power for Maddy.**
- **God has a plan and a purpose for Maddy's life.**
- **We don't control God's plan and purpose for Maddy's life.**
- **God sees what is going on and knows the truth.**

- **God loves Maddy more than we do.**

To this day, I look back at that discussion on our "date night" as a breakthrough. Kelly and I had literally spent months trying to be strong, but yet, we were both filled with worry. We had spent months trying to control things that we had no control over. That night, we, together, fully took a step back, realizing the error of our mindset. We recognized, as a couple, that it wasn't what we wanted that mattered. We accepted the fact that God's plan for Maddy may be different than what our plans would be or what we may have envisioned. This didn't mean we loved Maddy one bit less, but it meant that we realized God loved her more than we did. As we finally realized that for quite some time, we had been trying to control far too much, we asked God to work His plan, regardless of what it was. We trusted God. That evening, over dinner, we let go, and we found our faith.

After that evening, things changed. Rather than a sense of worry and fear that we might never see Maddy again, we both had a feeling of optimism. That may sound strange, but the optimistic feeling stemmed from the fact that Kelly and I had come to the conclusion, no matter what, God had a plan, and even if we didn't see or understand what that plan was, we knew it would be what was right for Maddy and for our family. We all loved that little girl and we wanted to see her again, to hold her again. It had now been six months since she had left. We longed just to visit and interact with her one more time, but, if it turned out that this was not what God had planned for Maddy and our family, we were OK with it. That didn't mean this experience, this foster child, this case wouldn't leave a scar in some way, but it did mean that we realized that God's plan was bigger than ours. With His help, we knew scars can heal.

So we moved forward, day by day and week by week. We talked with Breah, Jay, Aiden, Alex, Kate, Trey, and Joel. We really tried to share this new perspective with them, hoping they would understand what had taken Kelly and I far too long to realize. Simply put, they did get it, as was summarized by Kate during a family meeting one night. Kate made the perfect analogy as we all sat around the living room talking when she said, "You mean, it's kind of like God watches over us all, no matter where we are. We talked about that at school today. He watches over us at school and at home, and even if we are somewhere not with our family, He still watches over us. He watches over us even if everyone in our family is in different places." Exactly. I couldn't have said it any better myself.

With this new found attitude, our family moved forward. We didn't know what to expect or when to expect it. Nothing had been handed down yet from the Ohio Supreme Court regarding the *"opinion to follow"* that had been mentioned in their June announcement regarding our case. We were closing in on the day that final written closing arguments were due in the Allen County Juvenile Court regarding the Legal Custody case. We knew after these were submitted to that court, a decision would follow, but there was no way of knowing how long that decision would take. These were the circumstances that were present on September 20, 2016, when we received an unexpected notification. That day, the Ohio Supreme Court made an additional announcement in regard to our case saying, *"It is hereby ordered by the court, sua sponte, that all proceedings in the case captioned In the Matter of M.A.S, case No. 2014 JG 31779, in the Allen County Juvenile Court are stayed pending resolution of relators' motion for reconsideration."* Just as Mercer County Probate Court had been stopped from proceeding with Maddy's adoption case in June, Allen County Juvenile Court had now been stopped by the Ohio Supreme Court from proceeding with Maddy's Legal Custody case.

"You need to persevere so that when you have done the will of God, you will receive what he has promised." Hebrews 10:36

CHAPTER 20

A SUPREME DECISION

This new order from the Ohio Supreme Court brought about many questions, the most obvious of which was, aside from staying the court proceedings in Allen County Juvenile Court, what else did this mean? Initially, at least, it was comforting to realize, the case involving our adoption of Maddy was still being looked at and considered. Kelly and I thought about her every single day. Our hearts ached to just see her again, to hold her, hug her, and tell her we loved her. She was now almost 26 months old. Knowing she had no clue why or how her life had been turned upside down when she was removed from our home, we had prayed for months that God would watch over and comfort her. On many occasions in the preceding months, I had considered what I would have done differently had I known that we would not be allowed to visit with Maddy for such an extended period of time. Thinking about this really changed my perspective moving forward. I realized just how many moments I had taken for granted in the past. Losing someone you love so quickly makes you realize that we should never take one moment for granted with anyone we love. Each and every interaction, conversation, every moment with the loved ones in our life matters. We are never guaranteed tomorrow or "the next time" we will see them. This is a lesson I have carried with me ever since Maddy left our home. So, with that perspective in mind, I, personally, longed to see Maddy again, even if it were just for one more visit. There was so much I wanted to say to her, to tell her. Even knowing she was young enough that she would not understand or even remember the things I wanted to say, I knew she would feel the love of a father that I had for her.....even if just for that one more moment.

But, the Ohio Supreme Court had now again spoken. We had thought we were approaching the end of the Allen County Juvenile Court case for Maddy, in which legal custody would either be granted to Kelly and me or to Maddy's relative. Despite Maddy's birthmother's wishes, despite all the testimony that had been given supporting Maddy's placement with Kelly and me as her Legal Custodians, despite the concerning police reports, the denial of medical evaluation, despite all the things that we knew pointed to Maddy's best interests lying with placement in our home, we were not confident that we would be awarded Legal Custody. The actions of the court, the denial of visitation as this legal process played out, the ignoring of concerning evidence by both Allen County Children Services and the Allen County Juvenile Court all pointed to the conclusion that this decision was not going to go in our favor. Kelly and I had advocated for the best interests of a child that had been placed in our care. We had treated her no differently than any of our other children. We had been honest, vocal, and determined. We had stood up to the system, and the system seemed determined to put us in our place. After all, we were just foster parents. However, the Ohio Supreme Court had now put the brakes on this process that was playing out. We didn't know exactly what this meant, but we waited and we prayed.

Weeks passed, and we continued to wait for further instructions or an opinion from the court. As this time passed, we continued to travel weekly with Maddy's birthmother to her out-of-state visitation, and we continued to sit in the parking lot as Maddy visited with her birthmother. This process never got easier. To be so close to Maddy, but yet prohibited from seeing her, despite our requests and her birthmother's request, was agonizing each and every week. On October 18th, 2016, we traveled with Maddy's birthmother for the 27th out of state visit. Little did any of us realize this would be the last of these trips.

On October 20, 2016, we received the *"opinion to follow"* that had been alluded to by the Ohio Supreme Court back in June. This opinion stated in part,

Prohibition—Adoption—Probate court's authority to order preadoption placement pursuant to R.C. 5103.16(D) is within its exclusive, original jurisdiction over adoption proceedings even while child is subject to juvenile court's continuing jurisdiction—Probate court acted within its jurisdiction and in accordance with statutory authority in placing child for adoption with foster parents with mother's consent.

There it was…..the ruling of the Ohio Supreme Court stating that Mercer County Probate Court was operating within its exclusive jurisdiction in accordance with the Ohio Revised Code over adoption on March 31, 2016, in ruling that Maddy's birthmother knowingly acted in Maddy's best interests in applying to place her daughter for adoption, that Kelly's and my adoption of Maddy was in her best interests, that the adoption should proceed by ordering placement of Maddy back in our home. In an effort to stop her adoption, Maddy had been kept from us for over seven months by an agency and a Juvenile Court that were operating in defiance of Ohio law.

This ruling brought about an avalanche of emotions, the first of which was that of thankfulness for God's grace. I still remember receiving notification of this ruling…..it is a day I will never forget. At work, I quickly called Kelly and informed her of what I had just learned. We both sat on the phone that day crying, unable to speak because there were no words that needed to be said or that could encompass the emotions we were feeling. After 218 days, we would finally see Maddy again. Our daughter was coming home!

The rest of the day was a blur. Numerous phone calls were made to our family and friends advising them of what we had learned that morning. Many other phone calls were made to our attorney and to Maddy's birthmother's attorney coordinating how this process of Maddy coming home would work. The attorneys dealt with working out the details with Allen County Children Services officials. Obviously, Kelly and I were ready to drive out-of-state that day to get Maddy, but it wasn't that simple. By the afternoon, a plan was in place. Maddy would be coming home to us the following day, Friday October 21st, 2016, in the early afternoon. Agency officials were to go out-of-state to pick Maddy up, and would return to Ohio, where Maddy would be brought to her birthmother's attorney's office. There, at the office, Maddy would be greeted by her birthmother, and then brought back to a room where our family would be waiting. Knowing the loving bond that existed between Maddy and her birthmother, we felt it important that she be the first person Maddy would meet. Her birthmother had stayed a constant in her life through the months of out-of-state visitation. Having not seen Maddy for such a long period of time, Kelly and I both wanted her birthmother involved, being the first person to greet her. We were not sure how Maddy would react seeing us again. Would she remember us? Would she understand that we were back, this time for good? Maddy's birthmother reintroducing us to Maddy would bring stability, and that would be good for Maddy. So, with this in mind, plans were made for the following day.

Waking up the next morning, our entire family had a sense of anticipation. We could not wait for the afternoon to come so that we could see Maddy again. As we prepared to leave our home late that morning, the phone call we received came as quite a surprise. As I hung up the phone, the look on my face must have spoken volumes to Kelly, because before I could even start to explain what I had just been told, Kelly asked me, "What's wrong?"

The phone call had been from our attorney advising that, judging from facts that had started to present themselves, there may be "problems" with Maddy's return to us that day. The fact of the matter was that Maddy's relative had showed up in Ohio, searching for an attorney to represent her. The reason this was known was, out of all the attorneys that could have been approached, Maddy's birthmother's attorney, John Huffman, had been visited by this relative. As soon as she started to explain to him why she was looking for an attorney, he realized who he was speaking to. He advised her that he was already involved in the case, representing Maddy's birthmother, and she bolted out of the office. This interaction had generated a call to Allen County Children Services, who then tried to call Maddy's relative numerous times, without receiving an answer. So, it was with that as the background, that Kelly and I were asked to come to Lima and wait with Maddy's birthmother at the office of John Huffman as Allen County Children Services tried to make contact with and take possession of Maddy from her relative.

As Kelly and I headed to Lima, we continued to get phone calls updating us on the circumstances as they occurred. Through reaching out to other Lima area attorneys, it was quickly found that Maddy's relative had left John Huffman's office and headed to other attorney offices in search of legal representation. Numerous area attorneys confirmed that a woman matching the description had stopped by their office, only to quickly leave when advised that they were not going to take her as a client. At one area office, the attorney had been in a meeting so, Maddy's relative had said that she would stop back. It was now almost noon. This was the same time that Maddy was supposed to be handed over to Allen County Children Services officials in her out-of-state location. Agency officials were at the home, and confirmed that no one was there. Maddy's relative was still not answering phone calls to her cell phone. In consultation with both our attorney and Maddy's birthmother's attorney, the decision was made to involve Allen County Sheriff's Officers to "stake out" in unmarked vehicles the office of the attorney at which Maddy's relative had indicated she would be returning to. As time passed, she did not return.

In the Lima office of John Huffman, Kelly and I sat around a conference table with Maddy's birthmother by our side and prayed. As Allen County Children Services officials and representatives from the Allen County Prosecutors Office updated John Huffman, he relayed the information to us. Finally, in the early afternoon hours that day, a phone call was placed to Maddy's relative's cell phone. She did not answer, but we were told that a message was left indicating that if she did not return the call in a short period of time, she would be charged with felony kidnapping. Shortly thereafter, she did return the call, and was instructed to proceed to Allen County Children Services to deliver Maddy to agency officials. However, she indicated that she would not go there, that she did not have Maddy with her, and that she was returning to her out-of-state home. As Kelly and I received this news, a sick feeling filled the pits of our stomachs. We asked that an amber alert be issued. We sat in the room, listening as this request was conveyed by John Huffman,

147

and as this request was refused by Allen County Prosecutor Jurgen Waldick.

The rest of the day was a blur. For hours, no one knew Maddy's location. As this situation continued to play out, with Allen County officials refusing to issue an alert, our attorney took action in coordinating with Mercer County officials to get an amber alert issued. As you will remember, Mercer County Probate Court had issued an order on March 31st, 2016, for the immediate return of Maddy by Allen County Children Services. In coordination with our attorney, it was decided that an emergency hearing would be held at 4 pm that afternoon to re-issue the order directing both the agency and Maddy's relative to return Maddy, and that due to Maddy's relative's refusal to comply with the direction that had been given her, the Mercer County Judge would order an amber alert to be issued by the Mercer County Sheriff.

Shortly before this hearing took place that afternoon, we received a phone call. Maddy's relative had shown up back at her home. Maddy was with her. Agency officials had taken custody of Maddy and were enroute back to Lima to hand over custody at John Huffman's office.

That evening, as 7 o'clock approached, Maddy arrived at the office. As we had planned, Maddy's birthmother greeted her out front. Through the open office doors, we could hear Maddy exclaim, "Momma", and proceed with her 2 year old jibber jabber. That sound was music to our ears. Due to the circumstances of the day, we had left Kate, Trey, and Joel at home with family. Alex

148

was out of town with a friend, so Kelly and I waited with Breah, Jay, and Aiden in the office's conference room. We heard the footsteps as Maddy's birthmother carried her down the hallway, approaching the room where we were waiting. As she entered the room, Maddy in her arms, the moment we had been anticipating for months arrived. Maddy looked across the room, surveying the scene. After a few seconds, her eyebrows slowly began to rise as her big, round, brown eyes started to open wide. We all held our breath, not knowing what Maddy's reaction would be. Suddenly, Maddy pointed across the room to Kelly, exclaiming with great surprise and delight, "MOMMY"! Her birthmother set her down, and Maddy's short little legs propelled her across the office as fast as they could. She jumped into Kelly's arms. After 218 days, Maddy was home.

Maddy remembered each one of us. From Kelly, Maddy looked around the room. One by one, she ran to us all. "Daddy" was next as I hugged her tightly and she patted my chest like she had found a long, lost puppy. She next focused her attention on "Beeeeah", as she pronounced it at the time. Then came, "Jay", whose name was always easy for her to say. Finally, she finished her lap around the room, and hugged Aiden, or "Dindin" in her vernacular. Smiles saturated the room. As we prepared to leave that night, Maddy asked about "Axe" (Alex), Kate, Trey, and Joel, or rather, "Joel" and "Joel" because at that time, she called them by the same name. We told her that Kate, Trey, and Joel were waiting for her at home, but since Alex was out of town with a friend, we decided to FaceTime call him on the way home. Driving down the

149

streets of Lima that night, as Alex answered, we handed the phone to Maddy. "AXE!" she exclaimed, quickly followed by, "Hey!", like she was making sure she had his attention. She then finished by telling him, "All of us", like she was just trying to make sure he knew she was back.

Arriving home, Kate, Trey, and Joel and a welcoming party of family and friends were awaiting Maddy's arrival. Maddy entered our home and acted like she had never left. She headed straight for her toy box and started searching through it, furiously pulling out stuffed animals and baby dolls in an effort to find the one she was looking for. The homecoming that night was amazing, and God's faithfulness was shown in that Maddy re-entered our home like she had never been gone. Seven months had passed since she had last been in our home, her home, yet, to Maddy it was all summarized by one simple statement. In the words of this child, "All of us" had been put back together again.

"Many are the plans in the mind of a man, but it is the purpose of the Lord that will stand." Proverbs 19:21

CHAPTER 21

AN ADOPTION

The following week, with the Ohio Supreme Court decision in the books stating that Mercer County Probate Court could proceed with our adoption case, all stay orders were lifted. In response, on October 25th, the Allen County Juvenile Court ruled giving legal custody to Maddy's relative. In its decision, the court related how Kelly and I had acted against Maddy's best interests, highlighting that due to our vocal stance advocating for her and our social media campaign to bring her home once Mercer County Probate Court had issued the adoptive placement order, we had "let a genie out of the bottle" and that could never be undone. What the judge failed to acknowledge in his ruling was that, per the Ohio Supreme Court decision, the March 31st adoptive placement order issued by the Mercer County Probate Judge had given Kelly and me care, control, and custody of Maddy and that she had been wrongfully kept from us for over seven months by the actions of his court and Allen County Children Services. In addition, it was puzzling to us why the Allen County Juvenile Court judge would have issued the legal custody decision, and, in fact, our attorney questioned whether it was even a valid legal decision. The facts of the case as it stood were that Maddy was under Mercer County's Adoptive Placement Order. All that was left was Mercer County Probate Court's scheduling and holding of an adoptive finalization hearing. Our attorney felt that this Legal Custody ruling was only done in an attempt to give Maddy's relative some sort of legal standing in order to try to prevent the adoption from happening. So, consideration was given to appealing the Legal Custody ruling. However, in the end, it was felt that an appeal on the matter would just be a waste of money and time, because we now had physical custody and Maddy's adoption was going to happen soon.

As we moved into November, awaiting our Mercer County adoption hearing to be scheduled, Maddy continued to flourish. The months of clouds that seemed to hang over our home while she was gone were quickly replaced by the sunshine of her smile and the happiness of her giggle as she again daily roamed around the house like she owned it. The evening of November 1st, Kelly received a visitor unexpectedly. Mercer County's Prosecuting Attorney, Matt Fox, stopped by our home asking if he could come in to discuss something with us. I was out of town working that night, and unavailable, but Kelly welcomed him in, wondering what was going on as she noticed two Celina Police Department cars outside. He proceeded to inform Kelly that he had been called because Maddy's relative had shown up at various local law enforcement agencies requesting officers to accompany her to our home to remove Maddy from our care, claiming that we had her "illegally". Of course, in our county and in our home town, our case and the subsequent Ohio Supreme Court decision was very well known, so these law enforcement officials informed Maddy's relative that they couldn't do anything without a court order. Once she left, the county court officials were notified, which is what brought about this visit to our home. That night, Kelly was counseled to not leave our home for the remainder of the night and was told that a Police Department unit would be stationed to watch over our home. The following day, the Mercer County Probate Judge issued an order to all county law enforcement agencies and officers stating clearly that Maddy was not to be removed from our home per the adoptive placement order that had been issued by the court on March 31, 2016.

As we moved through the month of November, a court date was scheduled for December 9, 2016. Leading up to this date, an attorney who had been retained by Maddy's relative filed multiple motions in Mercer County Probate Court requesting a delay to the scheduled hearing date, objecting to our pending adoption of Maddy, and requesting to be made a party to the adoption. The probate court indicated that it was not going to delay the hearing any further, but invited Maddy's relative and her legal counsel to attend the December 9, 2016, hearing.

The morning of December 9, 2016, Kelly and I along with Maddy's birthmother and our attorneys attended the scheduled hearing in Mercer County Probate Court. With all the motions that had been filed trying to delay and/or block our adoption of Maddy in the preceding weeks, we expected that the judge would rule on those motions, then determine whether to proceed to schedule an adoption hearing. Arriving that day, we noted some unexpected persons to be in attendance for the hearing who were waiting outside the court room. These attendees included Farley Banks, Maddy's former guardian ad litem (GAL), who had done a complete flip-flop in the Allen County hearings, and Brent Bunke, the Allen County Children Services case supervisor who had overseen many aspects of the case and decisions of the agency with regard to actions (or inactions) they had taken with Maddy. Interestingly, as Kelly and I walked into the Mercer County court room, we deliberately looked at each of these individuals who would only stare at the floor as we passed.

The hearing commenced and the attorney retained by Maddy's relative was given the opportunity to explain to the court on what basis of Ohio law or previous Ohio case law his client had to request to be made a party to the adoption of Maddy and/or object to our adoption of Maddy. This attorney admitted to the court that he had nothing to cite. After this admission, the court did give Maddy's relative a chance to make a statement to the court regarding Maddy. Referring to the Mercer County Probate Court as being "unethical", she was warned that she should address the court with respect. So, after receiving this warning, she continued with a couple more sentences claiming that since Maddy was a blood relative, she should get her. That was it. The judge noted that he would take her statement under advisement, and since her attorney could provide no basis of law for the motions that had been made, the motions would be dismissed. The judge then dismissed both Maddy's relative and her attorney from the courtroom proceedings.

As the hearing went on, numerous individuals were again brought to the stand to be questioned by the court and testify on the record regarding our proposed adoption of Maddy. Maddy's birthmother tearfully testified that she knew our adoption of Maddy was in her daughter's best interest. Kelly and I testified regarding our understanding of what adoption meant and the responsibilities that came with it, our feelings and affection toward Maddy, and the mental and emotional pain our family had gone through during the time she had been taken away from our home. Rachel, a case worker who had done our home study for Maddy's adoption, testified regarding the environment she found during our home study, the interviews that had been done with our children and their feelings toward Maddy and our possible adoption, and Kelly's and my experience with adoption and readiness to be adoptive parents again. Molli Schleucher, an attorney who had been appointed by Mercer County Probate Court as Maddy's Mercer County GAL, testified regarding her interviews and visits with Maddy's birthmother, Kelly and me, and her unsuccessful attempts to meet with and interview Maddy's relative. She closed her testimony by making her recommendation to the court that she felt it was in Maddy's best interests that the adoption proceed. At the end of all this testimony, the Mercer County Probate Judge recited for the record the circumstances of this adoption case, the Ohio Revised Code sections, and the Ohio Supreme Court ruling in this case that gave the authority to the probate court to proceed with adoption, then asked Kelly and me if we wanted to have the adoption finalization hearing after a short recess, as long as we could bring Maddy back to the court room with us. We were shocked, but excited. We made calls to family and friends, and we called the kids' schools to let them know we would be there in short order to bring them with us to the finalization. A short while later, a small crowd had gathered in the Mercer County Probate Court room. Shortly thereafter, the Mercer County Probate Court approved our adoption of Madeline Anne. As the gavel dropped, there were smiles and tears all around. Our family now numbered 10 as Maddy officially became an Anderson.

CHAPTER 22

THE AFTERMATH

Following Maddy's adoption, our life seemed to return back to a somewhat normal pace, well, as normal as it can be for a household of 10. Gone was the worry, anxiety, and constant stress that that we had dealt with for over a year. Our whole family was able to move on and enjoy Maddy as an everyday participant in our lives. Having been through this whole ordeal together, and having all fought together for best interests of one little girl, Kelly and I and Maddy's birthmother continued meet for visits regularly. Kelly and I to this day feel it is an important aspect of Maddy's life that she knows her birthmother and has a relationship with her, so these visits have continued since Maddy's adoption day.

Christmas and New Year's was a great time of bonding and reflection. As we looked back on the year that had passed and all we had been through, we could not deny God's grace and blessing that had become so evident as we followed His plan for our lives and family. I would be the first to say, the path had not always been easy, but He had always been the rock that we could anchor ourselves to. There were times when we had wondered how we could go on, but those were the times when we had lost sight of that fact.

In late January 2017, Kelly and I received notification that an appeal of our adoption had been filed in the Ohio 3rd District Court of Appeals. Our attorney assured us that we had nothing to worry about. Her feeling from the start was that this appeal was being done more out of harassment to us than out of the thought that there was actually a chance to get our finalized adoption of Maddy overturned.

As we had already come to find out, answering this appeal would not be cheap or quick. There were numerous filings, counter filings, and briefs that would be submitted to the Court of Appeals over the ensuing months. Finally, in May of 2017, we were advised that a hearing in front of a three judge Appeals Court panel would be scheduled for June of 2017. At the appeals hearing, each attorney would have the opportunity to state their case and supporting Ohio Law in front of the appellate judges over the course of a fifteen minute timed presentation. Questions would be asked of each presenting attorney by the panel of judges, and the Court of Appeals would then take all the information presented as well as the documents filed in the case in account as they researched and made their decision on the appeal.

The hearing occurred on June 13, 2017. Surrounded by the support of family and friends, we arrived at the hearing that day wishing for an end to this ordeal, but confident that God was in control and Maddy was an Anderson as she was intended to be. The presentations were laid out, first by the attorney for Maddy's relative followed by our attorney's response. It quickly became evident that there was no basis in the law for this appeal. In fact, when questioned directly on this point by the panel of judges, the attorney who had filed the appeal admitted that while there was no Ohio law or case law to support his position, "this case is more complicated than that." He then went on to tell the judges that should he be unsuccessful in this appeal, he would be appealing this adoption on to the Ohio Supreme Court. As you would expect, the judges did not seem too thrilled by that answer.

Almost a month later on July 10th, 2017, we received notification that the 3rd District Court of Appeals had ruled in our favor, rejecting the appeal, and, thereby, upholding our adoption of Maddy. In the opinion, in part, the Court of Appeals stated, *"Framak does not point to any specific provision granting her the right to intervene in the adoption proceeding. Instead, Framak claims an interest in the adoption of M.S.A. because she was awarded Legal Custody of M.S.A. by the (Allen County) Juvenile Court. As such, Framak argues that her designation as M.S.A.'s Legal Custodian confers a statutory right to give or withhold consent to her adoption by the Andersons."* To Kelly and me, this blatantly exemplifies why, after the Ohio Supreme Court ruling came out allowing Maddy's adoption to proceed, the Allen County Juvenile Court judge attempted to award Legal Custody to Maddy's relative. However, the Court of Appeals went on to state, *"R.C. 3107 governs adoption in Ohio. R.C. 3107 contains no provision granting Framak a conditional or unconditional right to intervene in the adoption of M.S.A. Framak does*

159

not qualify as a person who must consent to the adoption of M.S.A. under R.C. 3107.06……..As such, Framak lacks standing to challenge the merits of the {Probate Court's} decision finalizing the adoption or the procedure it used."

In August 2017, the opposing attorney followed up on what he had stated in the Court of Appeals hearing and filed an appeal of our adoption of Maddy to the Ohio Supreme Court. More litigation, more court briefs to file, more harassment, and more expense was headed our direction. As our response brief was submitted in early September 2017, we did not know when to expect this to be over. After all, the last time we had been to the Ohio Supreme Court, it had been just over five months before we had received a decision in the case. This time would prove to be different, however, as on September 27, 2017, the Ohio Supreme Court by unanimous decision dismissed the appeal that had been filed. That long dark haired, big brown eyed little girl that had come into our home when she was just 14 days old – you know…..the one that was just supposed to stay in our home for a couple days – well, she would never again have to leave our home or our family. It was confirmed that day by the Ohio Supreme Court……all of us were Andersons.

"Before I formed you in the womb, I knew you……."
Jeremiah 1:5

CHAPTER 23

A CALL TO ACTION

A call to action can be defined as something done to provoke a response, sometimes an immediate response. As this book, our story, comes to a close, that defines my main objective in writing this book detailing the story of how our family was built.

I am thankful that God called my wife to action. She felt this initial nudge in her teenage years while serving on mission trips. That nudge turned into a calling as she grew older. I am thankful that she listened to God's call to action, for if she hadn't, our family wouldn't be the same. I am thankful that my wife called me to action. There was persistence, prayer, and, yes, some trickery involved, but without her calling me to action, our family wouldn't be the same. I am thankful that our children listened to Kelly's and my call to action and were openly accepting of that call, the dynamics it would change for our family, the added responsibilities it meant for each of them, and the sacrifices that each of them has had to make from time to time for each other as our family grew. Without their unconditional love, trust, attitude, and participation in the call to action, our family wouldn't be the same. Each and every one of them has made a difference in our family, each in their own way.

So with that being said, I am calling you, the reader, to action. I am not naïve enough to think that foster care is a calling for everyone, nor am I foolish enough to assume that all are called to adopt. Some of us are, however, and if you feel that nudge and that calling, then take action. Children throughout our cities, our counties, our states, our country, and our world are without a loving family each and every day. Without action being taken on our part, these children wait. Who will answer the call for them?

Bringing Alex home through adoption from Korea was not free. We spent just over $25,000 in his international adoption, but it was worth every sacrifice and every penny. In a little over a year of time through our adoption case with Maddy, Kelly and I were forced to come up with over $120,000 for legal expenses just to stay in the game. According to the law, we were right, but we had to litigate to enforce the law. We emptied our savings. We emptied our retirement accounts. It was still not enough. We were going against a government entity with limitless funds. Kelly and I would never have been able to afford the legal expenses involved with our case for Maddy if not for the outpouring of support we received from our family, friends, and community. Donations were given to attorneys, fund raisers and garage sales were held, pancake breakfasts and spaghetti dinners were scheduled. These acts of care and kindness by countless members of the community were the ONLY thing that allowed us to hang in there financially and stay in this case until the end. For those of you whose purpose does not lie in foster care and/or adoption, what can you do? You can support those families that are called to care for children through foster care and adoption. You don't have to be rich. It doesn't take large sums of cash reserves. Every little bit counts and adds up. Hold a fundraiser for a family. Organize a pancake breakfast or spaghetti dinner. And, if you can't provide support financially, then support these families through prayer, acts of kindness, and your time. Kelly and I have received all of the above types of support, and I can tell you, each one matters, they all make a difference.

Through our story, I hope it is evident to all that "the system" in place for children in foster care needs to be examined much more carefully. For this purpose, I am calling all of you to action. Take interest, ask questions, talk to your elected representatives, find a way to get involved because the system needs to change. Oversight needs to be implemented. Ask a foster parent in your community, who can they go to if there are concerns? Who is their advocate in the system to address their concerns as they advocate for the best interests of children placed in their care? My guess is that they will tell you they don't have an advocate and that concerns just have to be brought to agency officials. As exemplified by our experiences, this is an issue.

In light of these deficiencies, even before the outcome of Maddy's case was known to us, Kelly and I began working with our elected representatives to address what we feel are some of these areas of concern we have seen. In this endeavor, we have also become acutely aware that we can not take this subject lightly, for as we had draft legislation in process, a bill was introduced in Ohio that was directly conceived as a result of our Ohio Supreme Court case with Maddy. This bill, Ohio House Bill 283, if in effect during our litigation over Maddy's adoption, would have PREVENTED the adoption from happening. This legislation is the answer to the stand we took against "the system". It must be voted down and we must become active in ensuring that the system serves the best interests of all children in all cases, no matter what that may mean. The system, in some cases, has become more concerned with the ego and perceived power of the decision makers. The best interests of children must be put first and foster families, especially those with long term placements, should be given a seat at the table. So, I am calling every reader of this book to take action politically. Get involved. Talk to foster and adoptive families in your communities. Ask them what you can do in an effort to help improve the system in your county or state. There is no excuse for any of us to sit on the sidelines.

Looking back at our story, I think about the lessons I have learned along the way, and I ask myself what can be taken from our story? First and foremost, I would say my biggest take away is that God has a plan for each and every one of us. Just as God knew Breah, Jay, and Aiden would be our children, he also knew that Seung Joon Ha, born in Busan, South Korea, was destined to be an Anderson – as long as Kelly and I listened to His call. Even though they all didn't meet us for the first 3 to 5 years of their lives, God knew Kate, Trey, and Joel were also destined to be Andersons – as long as Kelly and I listened to His call.

And Maddy, the 14 day old baby girl who was coming to our house for the weekend, well, God knew it would turn out to be much more than that – as long as we listened to His call. God has a plan for each and every one of us, but for that plan to take place, we have to follow where He leads.

I have learned that faith is undervalued. In learning this, I found that it is easy to say that we trust God. It is much harder to actually put this trust into practical application. For quite some time, I thought I had faith and trusted God, but it wasn't until I let go of my worries and concerns, that I started to understand faith. And, it wasn't until I trusted God enough to understand it wasn't about what I wanted, but rather what His plan was, that I truly found out what faith was. In getting to this realization, I found that having true faith in God's plan is quite an awesome feeling that frees you from the worries of the storms we face in life.

I have learned the value of family. That may sound odd coming from a father of 8 children, but it is true. While my family is much different than many others, it is the perfect family. We have all come from different backgrounds, different histories, and different circumstances, but together God has made us into the large, assorted family unit that He chose. It has not always been easy, but I realize that Kelly and I have been blessed beyond our wildest imagination to be chosen by Him to lead this family. I pray daily that He helps me to be the husband and father that my family needs me to be for this family He has given. Too many times we place too much value in material things that won't last, not recognizing the true value we should be placing in our family that is forever. Children are a blessing and the legacy each of us leave behind. Never take the moments we share with them for granted and never undervalue what should be our most prized possession – the time we share with them and the impact we have on them.

Last, but not least, I have learned the value of determination. Stand up for what is right. Be a voice for the voiceless. Be an advocate for change. Don't be ashamed to accept help when it is offered. Don't be shy, the limelight is not always comfortable, but sometimes it is necessary. Fight injustice and don't back down. Don't pay attention to the odds or what people are saying. God is the only odds maker that matters – and He already has determined the outcome. We just have to stand up and do our part, and as we do our part, He will never fail us.

Thank you for taking the time to get to know our story......the story of all of us. Now take action in whatever way you are called, because children everywhere are depending on it!

ACKNOWLEDGMENTS

First and foremost, Kelly and I would like to acknowledge and thank our Lord and Savior, Jesus Christ. He chose us, we just followed His lead. It is only through His will, His plan, and His strength that our family has been completed.

Kelly and I would also like to thank all who have helped us along the way on the path to becoming the people and the family that we are. To be quite honest, there are far too many to name, and it is our fear that if we tried to recognize you all, we would be sure to forget some of you who have contributed to our family in so many ways.

To each and every one of you who have been there for us – you know who you are – THANK YOU! You gave us your prayers and encouragement in so many ways when it has been needed the most. Some of you we know very well, some of you are just acquaintances, and some of you we don't even know, but all of you have impacted the lives of Kelly and I and our children.

Lastly, I would like to say thank you to all my children – Breah, Jared, Aiden, Alex, Kate, Trey, Joel, and Maddy. Each one of you has played your own role in our journey to becoming the family that God wanted us to be. Each one of you has made sacrifices for the sake of others in our family. Every time our family has grown, you have all given up just a little piece of your mom and I so that there is enough to go around. Your sacrifices are appreciated. Your commitment to our family is recognized. Your strength through adversity is amazing. Children are our legacy that we leave in this world. You all make your mom and I proud! Don't ever forget a couple lessons that we have all learned together along the way:

There comes a time when we all must choose between what is easy and what is right.

ALWAYS DO WHAT IS RIGHT.

The best view comes after the hardest climb.

Never give up. God has a plan for us all, and your mom and I will always be there for you! We love you all more than you can imagine!